Ways In

Ways In

Approaches to Reading and Writing about Literature and Film

SECOND EDITION

Gilbert H. Muller
The City University of New York

John A. Williams
Rutgers University

Boston   Burr Ridge, IL   Dubuque, IA   Madison, WI   New York
San Francisco   St. Louis   Bangkok   Bogotá   Caracas   Kuala Lumpur
Lisbon   London   Madrid   Mexico City   Milan   Montreal   New Delhi
Santiago   Seoul   Singapore   Sydney   Taipei   Toronto

McGraw-Hill Higher Education ☄

A Division of The **McGraw-Hill** *Companies*

WAYS IN: APPROACHES TO READING AND WRITING ABOUT LITERATURE AND FILM

This book is printed on acid-free paper.

1 2 3 4 5 6 7 8 9 0 FGR/FGR 0 9 8 7 6 5 4 3 2

ISBN 0-07-251290-3

Publisher: *Steve Debow*
Executive editor: *Sarah Touborg*
Editorial assistant: *Anne Stameshkin*
Senior marketing manager: *David S. Patterson*
Producer, Media technology: *Todd Vaccaro*
Project manager: *Diane Folliard*
Production supervisor: *Carol Bielski*
Freelance design coordinator: *Gino Cieslik*
Photo research coordinator: *Jeremy Cheshareck*
Photo researcher: *Connie Gardner*
Cover design: *Gino Cieslik*
Front Cover Painting: *Vanessa Bell, "Interior with a Table," 1921.*
Typeface: *10/12 Palatino*
Compositor: *Shepherd Incorporated*
Printer: *Quebecor World Fairfield, Inc.*

Library of Congress Cataloging-in-Publication Data

Muller, Gilbert H., 1941–
    Ways in : approaches to reading and writing about literature and film / Gilbert H. Muller, John A. Williams.—2nd ed.
      p. cm.
    Includes index.
    ISBN 0-07-251290-3 (alk. paper)
    1. English language—Rhetoric. 2. Literature—History and criticism—Theory, etc. 3. Film criticism—Authorship. 4. Criticism—Authorship. 5. Academic writing. I. Williams, John Alfred, 1925– II. Title.
PE1479.C7 M86 2003
808'.0668—dc21
                                                     2002021274

www.mhhe.com

About the Authors

GILBERT H. MULLER, who received a Ph.D. in English and American Literature from Stanford University, is professor of English at the LaGuardia campus of the City University of New York. He has also taught at Stanford, Vassar, and several universities overseas. Dr. Muller is the author of the award-winning *Nightmares and Visions: Flannery O'Connor and the Catholic Grotesque, Chester Himes, New Strangers in Paradise: The Immigrant Experience and Contemporary American Literature*, and other critical studies. His essays and reviews have appeared in *The New York Times, The New Republic, The Nation, The Sewanee Review, The Georgia Review*, and elsewhere. He is also a noted author and editor of textbooks in English and composition, including *The Short Prose Reader* with Harvey Wiener and, with John A. Williams, *The McGraw-Hill Introduction to Literature* and *Bridges: Literature across Cultures*. Among Dr. Muller's awards are National Endowment for the Humanities Fellowships, a Fulbright Fellowship, and a Mellon Fellowship.

JOHN A. WILLIAMS, the Paul Robeson Professor Emeritus of English at Rutgers University, is the author of twelve novels, among them, *The Man Who Cried I Am* (1967), *Captain Blackman* (1972), *!Click Song* (1982), and *Clifford's Blues* (1999), as well as eight nonfiction works that include *Africa: Her History, Lands and People* (1963) and studies on Richard Wright and Martin Luther King, Jr. (1970) and Richard Pryor (1991). In addition, he has edited or coedited seven books, among them *The McGraw-Hill Introduction to Literature* (1985) and *Bridges: Literature across Cultures* (1994). A former journalist, Williams is also a poet, playwright, and librettist and a recipient of the Rutgers University Lindback Foundation Award for Distinguished Teaching, and awards from the National Endowment for the Arts and the New Jersey Council on the Arts.

To
Laleh, Parisa, and Darius
and to
Lori, Greg, Dennis, and Adam
and as well to
Margo, John Gregory, Nancy, and David

Contents

Part Two
THE ELEMENTS OF LITERATURE

Part Four
A GUIDE TO RESEARCH AND DOCUMENTATION

Preface

"Writing and reading are not all that distinct for a writer. Both exercises require being alert and reading for unaccountable beauty, for the intricateness or simple elegance of the writer's imagination, for the world that the imagination evokes."

Toni Morrison
Playing in the Dark

Ways In introduces students to the nature of literary and cultural inquiry. It highlights accessibly way the recursive nature of the reading and writing processes, while enhancing awareness of the relationship between a writer's personal voice and his or her culture. As a text bridging the gap between literary and composition theory, *Ways In* is a concise, integrated guide to critical reading, thinking, and writing about literature.

In this text we focus on the processes whereby students can explore the diversity of voices that they encounter in literature today. Many of the literary examples presented in *Ways In,* ranging from Sophocles' *Oedipus Rex* to the provocative sketch "Girl" by Jamaica Kincaid, reflect the multicultural ethos governing most contemporary literature anthologies. By stressing the many cultural contexts for composition, we root the reading and writing processes in considerations of race, gender, class, ethnicity, and region.

Because of its multicultural emphasis, *Ways In* can be a useful ancillary text for any literature course. Moreover, by engaging students in the actual stages of the reading and writing processes, while considering the basic elements of fiction, poetry, drama, and film, we offer a comprehensive guide tailored to the needs and expectations of today's diverse student population, which is a reflection of the United States. Strategies for making discoveries about literature (and discoveries about oneself) are given priority, from reading critically and responding to literature to planning, drafting, and revising compositions.

Throughout *Ways In*, students are encouraged to think about literature and then apply those discourse strategies appropriate to the critical tasks at hand. The text teaches students how to develop critical approaches to literature—whether feminist, historicist, psychological, reader-response, or any other—and how to apply this knowledge, as well as an understanding of the elements of fiction, poetry, drama, and film to their writing. We offer detailed guidance on the stages of the writing process, as well as explanations of personal, informative, analytical, and argumentative strategies for critical discourse. Examples of student and professional writing provide detailed guidance. From discussions of precis and summary writing to the writing of critical research papers, we attempt constantly to connect critical thinking and problem-solving skills to different writing situations.

The materials and methods of *Ways In* provide students with a text that they can relate to and that builds their confidence as writers in literature and combined literature-and-composition courses. The text emphasizes the reader's involvement with literature and authentic responses to fiction, poetry, drama, and film. It teaches students to deal wisely and well with the diversity of their literary culture.

We would like to thank our editor, Sarah Touborg, who has been gracious and supportive during all phases of the revision process. We also appreciate the assistance of Anne Stameshkin in coordinating the numerous initiatives and details involved in the revision of *Ways In*. Above all, we owe a profound debt to John Henry Davis at the LaGuardia campus of the City University of New York; an expert in film and a filmmaker himself, John guided us in our thinking about the new film chapter and prepared several drafts. Finally, several reviewers rendered valuable assistance:

Homer D. Kemp, Tennessee Technological University

Richard McLamore, McMurry University

Lynn Parker, Framingham State College

Elisabeth L. Cobb, Chapman Universty

William L. Knox, Northern Michigan University

Lisa Blansett, Florida International University

Barry Milligan, Wright State University

We are grateful for their advice.

Gilbert H. Muller

John A. Williams

PART ONE

Critical Reading and Writing

CHAPTER 1

Reading and Responding to Literature and Film

"The art of writing has for backbone a fierce attachment to an idea."

Virginia Woolf

Writing essays for college English courses—indeed for most courses—is a challenge. You must generate thoughts and opinions; harness and organize them; and transform these ideas into effective papers. The end product of this process should be an essay that reads clearly and expresses your insights and discoveries about a topic in a clear and convincing way. To facilitate this process, *Ways In,* a brief guide to writing about literature and film, will show you how to develop ideas and support them with evidence drawn from literary and visual texts and also from research. In the end, you will discover the wisdom of Virginia Woolf's observation that you need "a fierce attachment to an idea" to produce writing that will make a positive impression on your audience.

WHAT IS LITERATURE?

Although critics argue over the definition, what has come to be known as *literature* is writing in prose or verse that contains complex yet coherent ideas and meanings; deals with significant or universal issues; contains original and imaginative writing; and interests a large number of educated readers. As the celebrated Peruvian novelist Mario Vargas Llosa states, "Literature has been, and will continue to be, as long as it exists, one of the common denominators of human experience through which human beings may recognize themselves and converse with each other." Who decides if a work—whether fiction, poetry, drama, film script, or essay—meets these criteria? Admittedly, experts often decide the quality of any endeavor. But anyone can learn to study, analyze, discuss, and apply the specialized vocabulary of criticism to literature and also film.

Of course, there is also a subjective element in literary criticism. For instance, in eighteenth-century England, a definition of "literature" would have included philosophy, history, letters, and essays as well as such standard forms as poetry. Literary judgments are based on the age's personal taste and various cultural assumptions, even though such tastes have been molded by conventional standards. This is a bit different from being an expert in a less subjective field like sports. A sprinter who can run the 100-meter dash in 10.0 seconds is obviously top-notch while another who runs the same distance in 12.0 seconds would not be considered a world-class competitor. With literature, it is more difficult to be certain of your opinions about what is good or mediocre. However, if a work stands the test of time like Sophocles' *Oedipus Rex* or *Othello* by Shakespeare or Tolstoy's *War and Peace,* you may assume that generations of readers have returned to these works and found them personally meaningful and of literary merit. This quality of literature to endure is what the writer Ezra Pound was referring to when he stated that "Literature is news that stays news."

Today, however, there is much debate over the idea of the *canon,* that is, the body of work we believe to be deemed literature. Many argue that what is considered literature is merely the narrow-minded view of a group of like-minded individuals from a more-or-less similar social class, with homogeneous values, who share a similar outlook on life and art. In other words, why have certain literary works been accepted, read and taught over centuries, while others have either vanished or have been ignored? This argument embraces cultures, genres, and social classes. Nonetheless, newly discovered or rediscovered works often make for exciting and provocative reading; only the future will tell us whether they will enter the body of writing we call literature. Take the work of Kate Chopin. Her short stories, for example "A Respectable Woman," and novels like *The Awakening* were neglected for many years; however, a couple of decades ago, critics began to view her work as explorations of feminism that were ahead of their time, so that now her fiction is read and discussed widely. Or consider the case of Emily Dickinson. Virtually unknown while she was alive, today she is considered to be one of America's greatest poets.

READING AND THINKING CRITICALLY

To write intelligently about literature, you must first read actively and think critically about it. But why does literature require such reading and reflection? Good literature forces you to enter into a dialogue with it. The themes, style, content, meanings, and structure of true literature challenge you intellectually and imaginatively. Other forms of writing usually do not.

You *can* read a story or novel straight through for entertainment, sensing that you have easily extracted all its meaning, derived from it all its pleasure. This is popular literature—crime fiction, romance novels, westerns, science fiction—and you *consume* these forms. When you are done, you find yourself satisfied for the time being. You put the book down, often not to pick it up again. Conversely, with truly significant literature, you not only read it, but also think about it, ask questions about it. How do you know if what you are reading requires such an effort? If you find yourself thinking about what you have read; if you feel the need to review some or all of it for deeper comprehension; if there are elements such as character, theme, plot, style, and other literary components that have you curious or perplexed, the work is more likely to be literary.

Informed readers of literature usually automatically ask themselves certain basic, key questions about what they are reading. The following questions can help you grasp the significant elements of what you are reading and serve as springboards to pursue further and more detailed issues in the text.

1. What is the author's purpose?

A Raisin in the Sun has been viewed as one of the first plays that simultaneously brought the weakness and strength of the African-American family to light for mainstream America. Was that the purpose of Lorraine Hansberry, the playwright? Was the play's purpose to evoke sympathy, outrage, or was it meant to engage its audience in an evening of riveting theater, one that would make them raise issues about their own attitudes toward racism? Or did the playwright have in mind breaking racial stereotypes that many white Americans had about African-American families? All these would be valid purposes. But without the author directly stating his or her purpose, we must infer it. The value of inquiring about purpose is that it can assist you in understanding the *theme* of what you read.

2. What is the author's theme or main idea?

The theme of Raymond Carver's frequently anthologized short story "Cathedral" is that an individual whose perception is limited psychologically can be blind to reality while a truly blind person may have a rich experience of reality. If that statement seems emphatic, it was meant to be. It is one person's summing up of his interpretation of a work of fiction. The term "theme" is sometimes referred to as an author's main idea or major statement or "what the author is trying to say." Regardless of what term you use, you should be cautious in assuming that the theme *you* have determined to be the correct one is the only valid one. Of course, common sense and rational thought will prevent one from accepting *any* theme as possible; still, there may be more than one acceptable one. Stating your interpretation of a theme of a work of literature and then writing about it is an important step toward understanding what you read. It is often the starting and end point for making sense of a work of literature. Discovering a theme gives your reading clarity so that all the elements of what you read are more easily and succinctly comprehended.

3. What is the emotional effect of the writing?

Critics and philosophers have been concerned with the emotional effect of literature since the Greek philosopher Aristotle discussed the issue in his

Poetics some 2,500 years ago. He referred to the concept of *catharsis* as that emotion one experiences when watching a drama that purges one of pent-up emotions. Identification, anger, glee, sadness are all emotions that may be evoked by literature. In fact, tragedy and comedy, two modes of dramatic literature, are often defined by them. Your emotional response to literature will most probably be tempered by your own personality and life experience, perhaps even your gender. For years, critics called Hemingway a "man's writer" because his work portrayed stoic men who endured life without complaint. His story "A Clean, Well-Lighted Place" and novels like *The Old Man and the Sea* are fine examples of this tone of stoicism. Do you identify with the older waiter in "A Clean, Well-Lighted Place" or the old, solitary fisherman in Hemingway's novella? If so, how much has it to do with whether you are a man or woman? How much does it have to do with whether you yourself feel lonely or not and how you regard your loneliness? Raising questions about the emotional effect of writing helps you understand what you read and can assist you in understanding yourself as well.

4. What biases or ideological viewpoints do you detect?

Many students of literature claim that *all* authors have a personal bias and/or an ideological viewpoint that bears on their writing. For example, the mere fact that a writer has had a college education places him or her in a certain class, and therefore places that writer in a particular educational class. For your purposes, it is probably better to consider the bias or ideological leanings of a writer based on his or her gender; economic class; racial and ethnic background, and political viewpoint. Some authors present such viewpoints in more obvious ways than others. For example, Langston Hughes, an African American, was often critical of American society; if you read his poetry, plays like *Soul Gone Home,* and his short fiction, you will discover a humorous, lucid, and straightforward critique of class and caste. Similarly, when we apply such terms as Orwellian, Kafkaesque, quixotic, or Rabelaisian to literature, we use these words to capture certain characteristics of the human condition that Orwell, Kafka, Cervantes, and Rabelais reveal to us. Good literature often poses radical questions about the world in which we live.

5. What personal experiences and/or biases do you bring to the work?

The flip side of the author's bias is your own. You should not necessarily consider the word "bias" in this context a negative one. Rather, it is meant to denote your own perspective based upon your social, economic, and ethnic background. For example, if you are an African American and read the fiction of John A. Williams or August Wilson's plays, you are more likely to have a personal response based upon your racial heritage than if you are a white American.

Raising these questions (merely a sampling of the many you could ask) about what you read should demonstrate how literature challenges you, makes you wonder and question. True literature *requires* that you do this in order to derive full appreciation of it.

LEARNING TO ANALYZE LITERATURE

To illustrate the need to read literature critically, examine the following two passages. The first is a fictive episode; the second is a very brief story entitled "Girl" by Jamaica Kincaid. As you read the two passages, think about how they differ:

"You should be more tidy in your everyday habits," Janine's mother said sternly, as she examined her daughter's messy room.

Janine averted her eyes from her mother's severe gaze and uttered a deep sigh, as if to communicate that she had heard it all before.

"I want you to pay attention to me. I am your mother, and I set the rules for conduct in this house," her mother continued.

"Mother, why are you always lecturing me? The way I keep my room is my business. Patricia's mother lets her keep her room any way she likes. Besides that, she lets her stay out late, and gives her plenty of spending money." Janine was getting more and more frustrated.

Janine's mother was wishing her daughter would stop this endless comparison. She felt it undermined her authority.

"I'm not Patricia's mother. I'm your mother. And you're not Patricia, you're Janine, my daughter. Now I expect you to start following the rules around here."

• • •

Wash the white clothes on Monday and put them on the stone heap; wash the color clothes on Tuesday and put them on the clothesline to dry; don't walk barehead in the hot sun; cook pumpkin fritters in very hot sweet oil; soak your little cloths right after you take them off; when buying cotton to make yourself a nice blouse, be sure that it doesn't have gum on it, because that way it won't hold up well after a wash; soak salt fish overnight before you cook it; is it true that you sing benna[1] in Sunday school?; always eat your food in such a way that it won't turn someone else's stomach; on Sundays try to walk like a lady and not like the slut you are so bent on becoming; don't sing benna in Sunday school; you musn't speak to wharf-rat boys, not even to give directions; don't eat fruits on the street—flies will follow you; *but I don't sing benna on Sundays at all and never in Sunday school*; this is how to sew on a button; this is how to make a buttonhole for the button you have just sewed on; this is how to hem a dress when you see the hem coming down and so to prevent yourself from looking like the slut I know you are so bent on becoming; this is how you iron your father's khaki shirt so that it doesn't have a crease; this is how you iron your father's khaki pants so that they don't have a crease; this is how you grow okra—far from the house, because okra tree harbors red ants; when you are growing dasheen, make sure it gets plenty of water or else it makes your throat itch when you are eating it; this is how you sweep a corner; this is how you sweep a whole house; this is how

[1]Calypso or rock and roll.

you sweep a yard; this is how you smile to someone you don't like at all; this is how you smile to someone you like completely; this is how you set a table for tea; this is how you set a table for dinner; this is how you set a table for dinner with an important guest; this is how you set a table for lunch; this is how you set a table for breakfast; this is how to behave in the presence of men who don't know you very well, and this way they won't recognize immediately the slut I have warned you against becoming; be sure to wash every day, even if it is with spit; don't squat down to play marbles—you are not a boy, you know; don't pick people's flowers—you might catch something; don't throw stones at blackbirds, because it might not be a blackbird at all; this is how to make a bread pudding; this is how to make doukona; this is how to make pepper pot; this is how to make a good medicine for a cold; this is how to make a good medicine to throw away a child before it even becomes a child; this is how to catch a fish; this is how to throw back a fish you don't like, and that way something bad won't fall on you; this is how to bully a man; this is how a man bullies you; this is how to love a man, and if this doesn't work there are other ways, and if they don't work don't feel too bad about giving up; this is how to spit up in the air if you feel like it, and this is how to move quick so that it doesn't fall on you; this is how to make ends meet; always squeeze the bread to make sure it's fresh; *but what if the baker won't let me feel the bread?*; you mean to say that after all you are really going to be the kind of woman who the baker won't let near the bread?

Now ask yourself a few questions.

- Which of the two excerpts is more challenging to you, the reader?
- Which one is more intriguing and more original?
- Which one requires more thought, more *critical thinking?*
- Which requires a second reading?
- Which seems to have a unique style?
- Which has an authorial voice, something special that makes it stand out from other things you've read?

If you review the two selections, only "Girl" *requires* you to think in order to appreciate and understand it. For example, who is speaking and who is being spoken to in the second excerpt? In the first, it is all clear and obvious. The dialogue sounds familiar, and has probably been echoed in numerous stories to be found in magazines and in the drawers of would-be authors. In the second, however, things are not as transparent upon first glance. You must infer certain meanings based on what the author has provided in the way of tone, diction, and voice. In the first selection, the author is "telling" the reader how the character feels with such indicators as "Janine's mother said sternly" and "Janine was getting more and more frustrated." In the latter, the author is "showing" you. What is she showing? That is the key to the meaning of the short story. The fact that the story is written in the imperative mode, that its tone is stern, didactic, and commanding should indicate that the author is demonstrating what strategies are needed for survival among women who live in a specific culture, and how these strategies are transmitted from generation to generation. By figuring out how the speaker is feeling and what her relationship is to the person being spoken to, you arrive at an understanding of the selection.

Another critical issue an educated reader might pose is what *formal* aspects make "Girl" special. What is there about its style that sets it apart from other writing? For example, consider the issue of person. The latter excerpt is written in the second-person narrative or "you" form (implied but not stated since it is in the imperative mode). This in itself adds a bit of originality to the work, for it is probable that most if not all fiction you have read has been written in the first-person or "I" form, or the third-person or "he/she" form. (A complete discussion of this subject appears in the "point of view" section in Chapter 3.) But it is not enough merely to be original. You should also consider the purpose or effect of using the second person. Perhaps it provides a way for the writer to more directly imitate true conversation. If you compare the two excerpts, you will probably agree that the latter does seem to mirror the vibrant, continuous quality of speech, while the former seems a bit stilted and contrived, and perhaps worst of all, generic.

Yet another element of active reading is recognizing the author's use of language. Like spoken language, written language has rhythm, sound, tone, diction, imagery, and syntax. In the second selection, you may have noted the music-like quality of the speaker. This may be attributed to the Caribbean dialect and its intonations. For example, if you review the selection by Kincaid, you will notice the author employs such literary devices as alliteration (repetition of consonant sounds), assonance (repetition of vowel sounds), and inventive use of punctuation (the string of clauses held together by semicolons to keep up the movement of the language).

Originality, subtlety, concerns with the aesthetics of language: all three are good indicators that what you are reading is literature, and not just standard prose. Notable writers like Jamaica Kincaid are aware of and incorporate these aspects of language into their writing. And the more you read, think critically about, and write about literature, the more mastery you will acquire in identifying these and other components that enable literary artists to make significant and memorable statements about human experience.

DEVELOPING A CRITICAL PERSPECTIVE

The more you read literature, the easier it will be for you to spot those elements that are worthy of critical analysis and further study. If you read a poem, for example, you can base your reading and understanding of it on your past experience of thinking critically about texts you have already mastered. Reading the short poem "Wild Nights–Wild Nights!" by Emily Dickinson—after having read and analyzed "Girl"—should provide you with the skills to scrutinize and "decode" the poem as a more informed and educated reader. Take a few moments to read the "Wild Nights–Wild Nights!" in its entirety and reflect upon it:

Wild Nights–Wild Nights!
Were I with thee
Wild Nights should be
Our Luxury!

Futile–the Winds–
To a Heart in port–
Done with the Compass–
Done with the Chart–

Rowing in Eden–
Ah, the Sea!
Might I but moor–Tonight–
In Thee!

Thinking critically about the poem should now come easier. You should be able to raise and answer for yourself questions of narrator, voice, style, language, and syntax. An important aspect of being an educated reader is being able to ask appropriate questions on your own. You may ask yourself such things as what is the tone (emotional tenor) of the poem? Who is speaking? How is syntax used to contribute to the poem's effect? Note, for example, how Dickinson's use of dashes breaches the conventions of customary punctuation. Mentally rearrange the lines in a more typical way and compare the two renderings. What do you discover? Examine the phrase "Rowing in Eden." What does it imply? How does it fit into the overall message of the poem? What is the effect of the nautical imagery? It should be clear to you now that the more you know the method and "language" of literary criticism (a subject treated fully in Part Two of this text), the richer your experience of it will be, and the more discriminating a reader you will become. Ultimately, when the time comes to write about literature, you will have the critical tools necessary to forge your ideas and thoughts into a well-crafted essay.

WRITING ABOUT LITERATURE

Writing about literature adds a unique variable to the equation of an assignment for English class. In order to write about a poem, short story, novel, or play, you must read critically and understand the unique and peculiar aspects of literature. With such an understanding, the analysis, interpretation, and decoding of literature can become a more organized and often more rewarding activity for you.

When you write, you write for a reason or a purpose. The well-known British essayist, journalist, and novelist, George Orwell, addressed this issue in his famous essay, "Why I Write." In it, he enumerated the reasons he wrote. Among them were "the desire to seem clever," the "desire to share an experience which one feels is valuable and ought not to be missed," "to find out true facts," and the "desire to push the world in a certain direction." Perhaps the reason this essay has become a classic is that it articulates an important issue about writers themselves. Orwell was addressing the reason for and purpose of his own essays and fiction, but it may be just as fruitful to ask the same question of the type of writing you will be doing in this course (and perhaps in future courses and careers). While your motives for writing may not be as ambitious as Orwell's, an understanding of the purposes of writing about literature may help you address the challenge with more clarity and understanding.

Since the times of classical Greece, philosophers have created taxonomies to identify the various forms and purposes of writing. While these systems vary from theorist to theorist, the following list provides convenient categories and sample selections from your literature anthology to elucidate them.

Writing to Summarize

Summarizing requires that you distill the major aspects of a work of literature, for example, its theme, characterization, setting, tone, and the like. Summarizing is helpful in formulating what you believe to be the essential elements of what you have read, and communicating them to others. You may also think of summarizing as an exercise for the mind. It challenges you to think about and express succinctly what you have read. Thus, in writing an essay tracing the developments of African-American drama in the twentieth century, you might begin your discussion of August Wilson's *Ma Rainey's Black Bottom* to include its basic characters, setting, theme, tone, and mood. A summarizing paragraph might go something like this:

> *Ma Rainey's Black Bottom*, set in a makeshift recording studio during the 1930s, depicts the economic and artistic control of black artists by white producers through a series of vignettes that show the resentment felt by black musicians toward their employers and to each other, despite the fact that they have been selected to play backup for a leading singer of the period by the name of Ma Rainey. Their banter reveals feelings of oppression, hopelessness, self-deprecation, and desperation, and culminates in a violent and ultimately deadly confrontation between two of the musicians: one who advocates that the black man take greater control of his destiny; the other attempting to exploit the issue by devising music more to the white man's taste.

Writing to summarize is often an intermediate step in the writing process in that it can be a preparation to writing an essay comparing and contrasting different works of literature or classifying a particular work of literature for inclusion into a particular school or genre.

WRITING TO RESPOND PERSONALLY

Perhaps the very first way we responded to writing as children was emotionally, before we had criteria established for us as to *how* we were to respond or *what* we were to seek out in a text to respond to. When you respond personally, you are actually developing a thesis about what you have read, even if it is merely to demonstrate how you feel about a particular work of literature. Responding to a text personally puts you directly in touch with what affects you about a work of literature.

Writing to Analyze

Writing is a process where feedback plays a crucial role. When you analyze what you read, you can more succinctly express on paper the significance of what you have read. By the same token, writing itself often helps stimulate ideas that had not occurred to you or were existing in only an inchoate state. Writing to analyze often enables you to zero in on a particular aspect or feature of a work of literature. For example, reading, then writing an analysis of sexual and religious imagery in the poem "Wild Nights–Wild Nights!" by Emily Dickinson can make the experience of reading and understanding the poem a more profound one. Like all forms of analysis, writing an analysis of a work of literature broadens and deepens your understanding.

Writing to Compare and Contrast

You gather knowledge about a field of inquiry through study. The more you study, the more you are likely to gain expertise in your field of endeavor. Comparing and contrasting works of literature is perhaps one of the most salient ways of developing your ability to discriminate between what is good and bad; understand what is unique about an author's work; and discern differences between authors, literary styles, genre, and different periods of literary history. You may compare many different aspects of literature. Perhaps the most fruitful forms of comparison are those that you spontaneously or instinctively become aware of through your reading. For instance, you may discover common themes between two poems, two short stories, or two plays, and to enrich your discovery, choose to write about what you see are the essential similarities and/or differences between the two. For example, the poems, "Photograph of My Father in His Twenty-Second Year" by Raymond Carver and "My Papa's Waltz" by Theodore Roethke, relate the memory of a father by his son. Neither memory is positive, and much sadness and betrayal seem to be expressed by both authors toward their respective fathers. But on closer examination, Carver's portrait seems to have the more pathos and sympathy. Thus, in contrasting the two poems, you might generate a theme such as the following: "While both 'Photograph of My Father in His Twenty-Second Year' by Carver and 'My Papa's Waltz' by Roethke portray a father/son relationship absent of healthy emotional affiliation, Carver's portrait is the more tender, sympathetic, and kind." An essay presenting this thesis would be one that compares tone; however, comparison/contrast essays can also address style, ideology, theme, and culture.

Writing to Classify

You probably spend much of your waking life classifying: classifying types of professors, types of food, types of jobs, and so forth. The ability to classify is a vital part of your intelligence. It helps you to see connections, understand relationships, and hone your skills at discerning similarities and differences between people and objects. Classifying literature provides you with a means of organizing your readings and coming to conclusions about what you have read in terms of where it fits in to a particular style, genre, historical period, ideology, or theme. For example, your anthology is classified around genres: fiction, poetry, and drama. As an exercise in classification, see if you can derive a meaningful classification from some of the works you have read in your anthology. Remember, however, that there are innumerable ways to classify, but the fruitful ones provide you with a means of gaining insights and helping to appreciate more fully what you have read.

Writing to Present an Argument

When you see the term "argument" in a writing assignment, it usually means something similar to "prove" or "demonstrate." You do this in writing about literature through developing your main point, and then providing supporting evidence to prove your point. Presenting an argument when writing about literature is very similar to the way a lawyer argues a case in court. He or she presents the thesis—that his or her client is innocent—then provides the proof to demonstrate the truth of the argument. Take, for example, the well-known short story "The Lottery" by Shirley Jackson. Since its publication, critics and students have tackled its meaning through analyzing the nature of the community it depicts, the behavior of its characters, its setting, social relationships in the town, and other elements. Some critics say it demonstrates blind adherence to ritual, the evils of fascism, communism, and the deadly consequences of conservatism. Perhaps your reading of the story can provide a new argumentative approach.

Writing to Evaluate

You are probably familiar with writing that evaluates if you have ever read a movie review or a book review in your favorite paper or magazine. Many people turn to these reviews in helping them plan their entertainment if they feel they can safely rely on the judgment of the reviewer. When you write to evaluate, you are judging what you are reading. You are considering whether what you have read has merit or not. Evaluation, however, is a complex matter, and much personal bias goes into an evaluation. Perhaps the best way to write a competent evaluation of literature is to read as much of it as possible. For example, if you critically and carefully read selections in any literature anthology, you will probably come up with a few favorites. You can then return to these selections and ask yourself, "Why do I favor this selection over these others?" Writing to evaluate will help you understand what qualities are considered meritorious in literature, and at the same time help you understand yourself. Through analyzing which works of literature you prefer and why, you can discover your own literary tastes. To substantiate any evaluation, the writer must show through example how the work possesses various positive and/or negative attributes.

We shall continue to deal with some of these approaches in subsequent chapters. For now, it is important for you to know that writing about literature enjoys a long tradition. After all, Aristotle, the Greek philosopher, provided us with a study of dramatic literature in his *Poetics* over 2,000 years ago. From the age of classic Greece to the present, we have been writing about literature. The concerns and approaches of literary critics and interpreters have been greatly influenced and shaped by the political, social, religious, and ideological forces of their times. Given these variables, we can agree that there is no single meaning in a text. When you read a text, you interact with it to create those meanings that you plan to write about.

APPROACHES TO LITERATURE

Thus far, you may have noticed that we have discussed literature in general and several works in particular by focusing on the works themselves. A school of literary criticism that had its roots in the 1920s and flourished in the 1950s, often referred to as "The New Criticism," popularized the approach of centering all meaning of a work of literature based on what was written on the page. But if you think for a moment, it should be obvious that there are many other ways to examine a poem, a short story, or a play. For example, you could examine the biographical elements of a work of literature by studying the writer's life. Or, if you're interested in the works of Freud or Jung or Lacan, you might apply a psychological perspective to a work, trying to understand, perhaps, the unconscious meanings of a play or story. Actually, for the past quarter of a century, many approaches to studying and thinking critically about literature have emerged. Some have remained popular; others have diminished in their influence. Nevertheless, a brief cross section of these various methods can enrich the way you look at literature and expand the ways you think about it. The following summary is provided to give you a basic understanding of these different methods. If any of them intrigue you, it is easy to follow up your interest by asking your instructor or by referring to the literary criticism of your library or on an Internet site.

Psychological Criticism

You are probably familiar with the concept of interpreting dreams. You may relate a dream to a close friend, and together try to figure out what the symbolism might signify. This activity is similar to the methods used in psychological criticism. This form of criticism attempts to apply modern psychological theories, primarily Freudian (and more recently Lacanian), to understanding literature. Freud, after all, in *The Interpretation of Dreams* explains what he terms the Oedipal complex by analyzing Sophocles' play *Oedipus Rex*. There are various ways that you may critique a work of literature from a psychological perspective. As noted above, you may take a work that has obvious symbolism and interpret what each image means. Another use of psychological criticism in literature is to attempt to understand the underlying motivations of a character in a short story or novel. What are the unconscious wishes of the characters in a play or work of fiction? Or what desires lie hidden in the relationship between Hamlet and his mother? Psychological criticism has also proved fruitful in examining so-called stream of consciousness writing, where we purportedly are entering into the mind of a literary work's narrator, as for example, we seem to do in the poem "The Love Song of J. Alfred Prufrock" by T. S. Eliot. Authors who have used this device in novels include such notables as James Joyce, Virginia Woolf, and William Faulkner. A third function of psychological criticism may be to understand an author's psyche through a study of his or her works. For example, many critics claim you can infer Hemingway's psychological makeup by reading his stories. If you have read his "A Clean, Well-Lighted Place," what sort of man would you believe had written it, and what are his values?

Historical Criticism

Historical criticism attempts to study literature by placing it within the context of the time in which it was written. Thus, styles and forms of writing may be historically based. Much of Shakespearean drama is written in blank verse, as in *Othello.* However, you would be hardpressed to find a contemporary play written in verse today. Most likely, we would think the author was being either old-fashioned or naive. Content as well as style is greatly influenced by historical forces. If you read Matthew Arnold's "Dover Beach" without a knowledge of the changes in European culture at the turn of the twentieth century, you cannot hope to understand many of the poem's references. The same holds true for William Butler Yeats' "Easter 1916." You must not only be aware of the Irish Liberation Movement to appreciate the poem, but you must have some inkling of the personages referred to throughout the poem.

The New Historicism

New Historicist critics take the concept of history and give it a new perspective. These critics argue that indeed literature can be studied from a historical point of view, but you must be careful not to inject your own historical perspective into a text that was written in another century. For example, the issues of jealousy raised in *Othello,* the issues of incest raised in *Oedipus Rex,* or the issues of the American dream addressed in *Death of a Salesman* may seem familiar and obvious to us. They might appear typical subjects for an afternoon TV show, in fact. However, the significance of the themes in these plays must be considered within the social, economic, political, and aesthetic contexts of the time they were written. *Death of a Salesman,* for example, opened the eyes of a generation to the reductionist, distorted view that the goal in life was to make a good impression on others, and to the need to make as much money as possible to prove your self-worth.

Biographical Criticism

Biographical criticism bears some similarities to historical criticism, only its concerns focus more on the particular life of the author, rather than the time he or she was writing in. Knowing that Wilfred Owen witnessed the horrors of World War I can help us understand the motivation behind the subject matter and themes in his poems, for example, "Anthem for Doomed Youth" and "Dulce et Decorum Est." Many poems cry out for biographical understanding of the author, for example Raymond Carver's poem "Photograph of My Father in His Twenty-Second Year" or Sylvia Plath's "Daddy" or Dylan Thomas's "Fern Hill." Prose fiction too lends itself to biographical criticism, as with "Girl" by Jamaica Kincaid. This is not to suggest that a work of fiction is a direct transcription of an author's life, but many authors use their experiences as sources of their richest work.

Marxist and Social Criticism

Although the philosopher Karl Marx wrote his major works in the nineteenth century, many literary critics have used his analysis of class conflict to examine even the earliest forms of literature. Perhaps because issues of class conflict seem to have existed at all times in human history (there were strong class divisions among the Greeks, for example), and since literature is often about people in conflict with one another and with society-at-large, Marxist criticism lends itself quite readily to explanations of much literature. Although issues of race and ethnicity are implicated in much modern literature, many stories and plays can simultaneously be interpreted using a Marxist paradigm. Even if the theories of Marx are not applied directly, the importance of power between and among individuals and groups, and the powerful influences of the conventions of society over our behavior tend to have at least some relevance to a Marxist reading. Much of Richard Wright's fiction subtly shows the potentially insidious effects of class and racism on the future of one young man. Just as graphically, Berthold Brecht's plays can be read as studies in the effects of sanctioned economic inequality on human beings and entire societies.

Structuralism

The literary method of structuralism takes its inspiration from the work of Ferdinand de Saussure, a Swiss linguist whose major ideas were transcribed by his students at the beginning of the twentieth century. The basic thesis of structuralism is that language is a system, a code of communication with its own rules and regulations. For example, sentences in English have a particular syntax which, if broken, ruptures the sense of the language. Literary critics have taken this basic idea and applied it to literature, primarily in their attempt to raise the importance of genre as an explanatory principle in discussing works of literature. For example, a structuralist might read a detective story, and rather than discuss merits of the style or the symbolic significance of the locale, use the story as a tool to understand the conventions of detective story type. Therefore, structuralist critics are often interested in examining works of literature to understand literature as a whole. So, for example, reading "The South" by Jorge Luis Borges, a structuralist might be more interested in discussing the concept of initiation and relating this concept to other works where initiation plays a significant role. Many advocates of structuralism have claimed that the idea of quality in literature must be reconsidered. Rather than ask whether a poem or story or play is well-written, the question a structuralist might ask is "how well does this work of fiction fulfill the conventions of the genre it is a member of?"

Reader-Response Criticism

If a tree falls in the forest and no ones sees or hears it, has it really fallen? This old riddle bears considerable significance to the school of reader-response criticism. People who advocate this approach to literature claim that a play or story or poem only exists in its relationship to the reader. Without the reader, it is not literature. The one who reads fulfills an essential aspect of the literary process. While this may seem rather obvious, reader-response criticism was an important reaction to the strong tendency of some critics—particularly the New Critics mentioned earlier—to consider the text in isolation, as though it were an immutable thing whose essence could be uncovered if one simply had the right tools and perspicuity. But reader-response critics hold that we construct meanings from what we read based upon our own individual experience, our cultural background, and the "community" within which we operate. You are a college student, for example, and you constitute with your peers a community. Your study of literature is obviously being influenced by the views that the academic community holds in so far as the way literature should be examined. Even your class itself may have its own biases toward interpretation (most likely controlled by the instructor or perhaps the philosophical perspective of your English department). That a text is incomplete in itself, and that reading it makes it come to life, gives more power to the reader, and some reader-response critics place as much if not more importance on the role of the reader as they do that of the author. Suppose, for example, your father works as a traveling salesman. This may have quite a bearing on your response to the play *Death of a Salesman.* Your response to any of the selections in the anthology may be strongly determined by your own class, racial, and ethnic background. Or take something even more basic: your gender. Chances are that male and female students may see a work of literature quite differently. After reading the story "The Lady with the Pet Dog" by Chekhov, your focus on character might be a result of how you identify with the characters, and that identification may well be based on your sex.

Feminist Criticism

Feminist criticism is an outgrowth of the feminist movement that began in the 1960s, but has been used retroactively to examine works wherein gender issues are prominent. In fact, feminist critics often uncover issues of gender in older texts that previously may not have been considered literature that had feminist implications. One major and legitimate complaint of feminist critics has been that women writers have been ignored since it has been mainly men who have ruled on what is considered literature and what is not. Feminist critics have adopted many writers that have lived in obscurity, so that today authors like Kate Chopin and Charlotte Perkins Gilman and Zora Neale Hurston have been recognized as major writers where formerly their works went unread. Feminist critics often look for and find themes of women's oppression, and stories by such writers as Kay Boyle, Alice Walker, and Nadine Gordimer are seen as works that not only examine women's lives but advocate for them.

INTERPRETING LITERATURE

In a class full of literature students, there is a strong possibility that there will be many interpretations of the same literary work. At the same time, the teacher's interpretation may differ from the students'. Who determines which is the correct interpretation? Or is it safe to say that there is more than one correct interpretation? Literature is open to so many readings, interpretations, and opinions that readers seldom agree on *every* aspect of a literary work. One may say that there are various competent readings, but not *all* readings are valid. You may even change your mind over an interpretation of a particular poem or story depending on when you read it, how often, and in what context.

Regardless of your personal interpretation of a story, it is most probable that the more carefully you read a work of literature, the more likely your interpretation will be valid. If you believe you understand the theme of a work, the particulars of it must back up your comprehension of it. The theme or meaning of a work is a generalization; the elements in it are the particulars. Put another way, your interpretation of a theme is your argument; its various elements are your proofs. If the proofs don't follow, then chances are you have a weak argument.

Some works are easier to interpret than others, however. The play *Krapp's Last Tape* by Samuel Beckett, for example, has been analyzed, studied, debated, and interpreted over and over. On the other hand, a play like *Suppressed Desires* by Susan Glaspell is fairly direct in its presentation of its theme, and few major arguments over its meaning are likely to be forthcoming. There are quite a few factors that influence the difficulty of interpretation of a work of literature. Two major ones are the degree to which the work breaks the conventions of genre; the other is the degree to which the motivations and/or the actions of a character are ambiguous. There have been many classroom arguments over whether the main character in Richard Wright's "The Man Who Was Almost a Man" actually becomes a man by escaping the provincial town he is living in or whether he is merely running away from his problems and therefore remaining a boy.

EVALUATING LITERATURE

"That was a really good movie!" "I couldn't stand the play we read in class." "I hate poetry." These common assertions are all evaluations. However, they are not particularly articulate ones. To evaluate or judge a work of literature requires that you have a set of guidelines. Guidelines for evaluation are not etched in stone, and depending upon your philosophical bent, can vary greatly. For example, a social critic might evaluate a work of literature depending upon whether it reflects the individual's own world view. If you've gone to the movies and have seen the "good guys" win, you may decide it's a good movie because it ended the way you wanted it to or anticipated.

In most English classes, however, evaluation is usually focused on the integrity of the work itself:

- Do all the elements seem to fit together in a cohesive unit?
- Do the characters seem plausible?
- Are the language, tone, and diction consistent, or if they aren't has the author provided a good reason for the inconsistency?
- Does the work seem to have an original voice, or like the example of "Janine and Her Mother," does it seem to be generic?
- Are the ideas in the work consistent?
- Does each element seem to contribute to the overall theme?
- Is the language vivid, appropriate, and accurate for what the author is trying to convey?

These are only some of the questions you should ask yourself when evaluating literature. For example, if you read poetry by Langston Hughes, ask yourself whether the diction and tone seem to ring true. Perhaps one way to summarize these questions about evaluation is to ask yourself the question, "Does the author of this work seem to have an intimate grasp of the universe of the poem or story or play?"

The more you read and ask questions like these, the more you will develop your own evaluative skills, and not have to rely on the views of others. We will return to these issues of interpretation and evaluation in several subsequent chapters.

CHAPTER 2

The Writing Process

*R*eading literature and writing about it are two closely related processes, so much so that the skilled reader of literature should always read with a pencil in hand, and mark the text in order better to understand it. (If you are working with a library book, make a photocopy of the material so that you can mark it without destroying someone else's book!) In literature, language is often compressed, or squeezed tightly into a shape or *genre* (meaning kind or type). Reading with a pencil is a tool that helps you to separate gently the layers of meaning. The process of writing about literature helps you to examine these layers one at a time in a formal and disciplined way so that your reading can be shared with others. In this unit we will look at the steps a reader takes in order to become a writer.

HIGHLIGHTING AND ANNOTATING THE TEXT

Let's take as an example the short story by Jamaica Kincaid, "Girl." The first step is to *read* the piece through at least twice. Next, read with a pencil. As you read, use the pencil to:

1. Circle key words (words that you do not understand, words that are repeated, for instance).
2. Underline lines or phrases that relate to the theme of the chapter, in this case children and families.
3. Annotate by asking questions in the margin about what the writer means or to record your own responses to the writer's words.
4. Highlight key phrases: "this is how" is repeated, so it might be important; the word "slut" seems powerful and stands out; related words like "sew" and "button," "buttonhole," and "hem" tell what the speaker is talking about.

The Writing Process

*R*eading literature and writing about it are two closely related processes, so much so that the skilled reader of literature should always read with a pencil in hand, and mark the text in order better to understand it. (If you are working with a library book, make a photocopy of the material so that you can mark it without destroying someone else's book!) In literature, language is often compressed, or squeezed tightly into a shape or *genre* (meaning kind or type). Reading with a pencil is a tool that helps you to separate gently the layers of meaning. The process of writing about literature helps you to examine these layers one at a time in a formal and disciplined way so that your reading can be shared with others. In this unit we will look at the steps a reader takes in order to become a writer.

— simple, domestic task

(this is how to sew on a button; this is how   *repeated phrase*
to make a buttonhole for the button you have
just sewed on; this is how to hem a dress   *rhythm of repetition*
when you see the hem coming down and so to   *unusual word!*
who is _prevent yourself from looking like the slut I
"you"?_ know you are so bent on becoming; . . .   └── *who is the "I"?*

You should read the entire story in this way, circling new words like
"benna" and "dasheen." Next, use a dictionary or a glossary to find the meanings of words you do not know. The word "slut," for instance, appears in the
Oxford English Dictionary with several meanings, including:

> "A woman of a low or loose character; a bold or impudent girl; a hussy, a jade."

Where would you look for the definition of words like "benna" and "dasheen"
if these were not in your standard American dictionary?

TAKING NOTES

Once you have carefully read the work several times, and highlighted and annotated as much as you can, the next step is to begin taking notes to help organize your impressions of the work so you can develop a *thesis* for your essay.
Notes can include:

- Listing
- Asking Questions
- Brainstorming
- Developing Subject Trees
- Keeping a Journal

Listing

Listing is the most familiar technique for organizing thoughts. We all make
shopping lists or lists of friends to invite to a party or names for sending out
Christmas cards. When writing about literature, the list might help put ideas
into categories. If your subject were "Girl," you might begin with a "do" list
and a "don't" list:

Do: wash clothes on certain days; cook fritters in oil; sew buttons on; walk
like a lady; love a man.

Don't: speak to "wharf-rat" boys; walk like a slut; pick other people's
flowers; be the kind of woman the baker won't let squeeze the bread.

Or you could list whatever has struck you as significant in your reading, and then review and evaluate what you have listed to see if any common theme has emerged.

Here is a typical list generated by one student on her notebook computer.

1. The imperative tone of the story shows a rigid system of parental authority in place, nothing like modern families in America today.
2. Many of the specific references in the story indicate the presence of a particular West Indian culture, for example, "pumpkin fritters," "don't sing benna," "wharf-rat boys," "dasheen," "doukona," etc.
3. The cultural milieu is one in which the types of directives the mother presents to the daughter are traditional female ones involving such activities as cooking, sewing, cleaning, housekeeping, and so on.
4. The mother also displays a traditional set of values by trying to instill in her daughter the proper comportment to assume around men.
5. Folklore and superstition are also replete in the lore which the mother is transmitting to the daughter, providing further evidence of a traditional culture; for example, she instructs her "how to throw back a fish you don't like," "don't throw stones at blackbirds," "how to spit up in the air if you feel like it."
6. Religion is another significant cultural value which the mother tries to instill in her daughter; for example, she says "on Sundays try to walk like a lady," "don't sing benna in Sunday school."
7. Above all, the mother displays the typical attitude of any mother who lives in a traditional culture and whose role it is to instill in her daughter the conventions and mores of her culture.

The function of listing is to generate ideas that ultimately can be used to help you organize the first draft of your essay.

Asking Questions

What pattern do the lists reveal? What insight into the story's meaning do the "do" and "don't" lists offer? The next step is to ask more questions, including who, what, and why.

Who is speaking in the story "Girl"?

To whom is she/he speaking?

How do we know?

Why are the sentences so long?

What is the tone of the speaker's voice?

Why are there so many domestic details about food and behavior?

Are there any clues to the gender of the speaker and the listener?

Does the language limit the story to one time or place, or is it universal in its meaning?

Does this work remind me of any others that I have read?

Brainstorming

Brainstorming is another way to generate ideas for a paper. Brainstorming can be done by yourself, but it can also be done in a group with two or three students who have all read the same story or poem.

- Sit in a small group.
- Have one member of the group read the story or poem out loud.
- Then let everyone offer his or her own insights into the meaning of the poem.
- Assign one member to record all of the responses.

Your brainstorming might result in a page that looks like this:

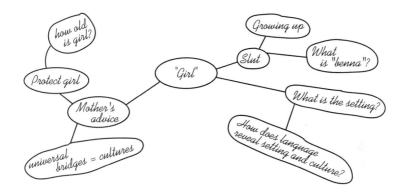

Working with a group, you may find that the ideas of other classmates, whose backgrounds are different from your own, help you identify special features of the story you might have overlooked.

Developing Subject Trees

Developing subject trees is another way to think about the story. From the "trunk" of the story "Girl," you might branch out into topics:

a mother's advice to her daughter

women's writing

do's and don'ts about sex

domestic details

unusual language: how does the writer convey cultural identity through details and local language?

etiquette books; Dear Abby; Miss Manners; giving advice: how is the mother's monologue like a "Dear Abby" letter?

Keeping a Journal

Keeping a journal is another way to record your ideas about a work of literature. You can use pages in a looseleaf, or keep a separate notebook. Each time you read a new story, start a new page and jot down your impressions of the work. Let yourself use all of the techniques—listing, asking questions, brainstorming and subject trees—to record your impressions. You will find that when you want to write a paper, glancing back at journal entries makes finding a topic easier. A journal page might look like this:

> A mother seems to be speaking to her daughter about all sorts of chores and different kinds of behavior. What to do and what not to do is the subject. The mother talks nonstop. It's as if she is giving the "girl" a lifetime of advice in one lecture. I can almost see the mother: maybe she's hanging clothes on a line in the hot sun and the daughter, she's about twelve, is following holding a basket of clothespins. The two work together and the mother talks as she hangs the sheets. I say the girl is about twelve because the mother uses the word "slut," so she's already worried about her daughter hanging out with boys and getting into trouble. What's funny is that even though it sounds like the mother is just rambling, when I read the story again, it was like there was a rhythm to it, and a whole lifetime of experience. I don't know what "benna" is, but whatever it is, the mother doesn't seem to like it much.

SELECTING AND LIMITING THE TOPIC

Once you have read the work, discussed it with your teacher and classmates, highlighted, annotated, and taken lots of notes, you are ready to find a topic for your essay. One way to select a topic is to ask questions and then write out a tentative answer. You can use the questions you asked while taking notes, and expand these with key words from the brainstorming session and the journal entry.

Who is speaking, to whom, about what?

The mother gives her daughter womanly advice.

Possible topic: something about mother-daughter relationships.

Once you have some ideas, the next step is to narrow the topic, or limit it, so that it is manageable in an essay of about 500 to 750 words. Some inexperienced writers think that keeping the topic very broad, like "women writers," makes it easier to write because they won't run out of material. But more experienced writers know better. The more you can limit the topic, the easier it is to support and organize the essay.

Broad topic: Women writers

More limited: Women writers' use of details

Even more limited: use of domestic details by African-American women writers

After you have a sufficiently limited topic, you can begin to plan and write the essay, using the following steps:

- Developing a Thesis
- Considering Audience and Purpose
- Revising and Editing
- Submitting the Final Manuscript

DEVELOPING A THESIS

Developing a thesis or main idea means that you have to decide what you want to say about the limited topic. The *thesis* is the most important part of the essay, for the thesis controls the plan for what follows. The thesis gives the reader your point of view or opinion on the limited topic. It may also suggest which strategy you plan to use to organize the body of the essay.

If your limited topic is use of domestic detail by African-American women writers, you can create a thesis by asking, what do I want to say about this topic? What do I mean? What is my purpose in writing the essay?

You can begin, as you did earlier, by asking questions.

Why am I interested in this topic?

What is unique or special about it?

What did I think about when I read the story that led me to this topic?

Do I like the story? Why or why not?

What about the story relates to the theme of children and families, and how does the story reflect on the multicultural themes of the other readings?

Sample thesis statements:

1. In her story "Girl," Jamaica Kincaid uses an accumulation of domestic details to reveal a mother's strict but loving concern for her daughter.
2. The mother in Jamaica Kincaid's story "Girl" cannot speak directly of her love for her daughter, so she uses details about a woman's everyday life to convey her pride and anxiety about her daughter.

Statements can be refined and expanded as you develop your ideas. The next step is to consider your audience and purpose.

CONSIDERING AUDIENCE AND PURPOSE

Who is my audience? In what way will knowing who the audience is shape my essay?

Why am I writing the essay? How will my purpose help me to choose a strategy for outlining the essay?

Your immediate audience is the instructor and your fellow students. At the same time, you are writing for a wider audience, the educated common reader, which might include anyone who has read Kincaid's story and wants to understand it better. Since your audience is a college audience, your writing will have a more formal tone than it might if you were merely having a conversation about the story with a friend. This tone is connected to the *purpose* of the essay. One purpose in writing is to help yourself analyze your own thoughts about the story by putting them down in writing. Another purpose, however, is to train yourself in a particular discipline, in the skill of college-level expository prose. By writing about literature in a college course, you are learning the conventions, or the rules and practices, of the world of professional writers. You are polishing your formal language skills and your skills in thinking and analysis in preparation for whatever career you will choose. Writing about literature, then, requires planning and attention to detail.

You can begin, once you have read the story, annotated it, taken notes, limited the topic and developed a thesis, and considered audience and purpose, to write the first draft.

WRITING AND REVISING

In order to write the draft, you can start with a simple outline:

Introduction, with thesis

Body paragraphs, with quotations from the story to support the thesis, normally using one of four major types discussed in the previous chapter: personal, analytical, comparative, or argumentative

Conclusion

In order to develop the body, you can decide which essay plan is best suited to the thesis.

- Is this a *personal essay?*
- Is this an *analytical essay?*
- Is this a *comparative essay?*
- Is this an *argumentative essay?*

Types of Essays

Read each sample essay and examine the writer's techniques. Then you will be ready to decide which strategy is best for the essay you want to write.

Personal   As mentioned in Chapter 1, this type of essay allows the writer to speak in her own voice, and to relate the literature to her own experience. The essay may use analysis or argument, but the focus is on the personal. For instance, a personal essay on "Girl" might be written by an African-American woman who grew up in Barbados and moved to New York, and who identifies with the experience in the story now that she is raising her own daughter. In writing her draft, this student can talk about "Girl" by connecting Kincaid's story with her own life. Or, as in the sample essay that follows, the student uses his own voice to record his impressions of Elizabeth Bishop's poem, "Filling Station."

Sample Essay: Personal

Cars and traveling by car have been part of the American identity since the first car rolled off an assembly line. To many ears, the names of cars are a genre of American poetry: Mustang, Firebird, Impala, Thunderbird, Dart, Seville, Imperial, Galaxy, Eagle, New Yorker. I always wished I could get a job dreaming up names for new models of cars. It's probably not hard to explain why a poem called "Filling Station," by Elizabeth Bishop, made me nostalgic for the days before gas stations became hygienic self-service supermarts without any style or poetry.

"Filling Station" is a description of an old-fashioned gas station, family run, where grease and oil are soaked into every surface. The poem begins with the speaker at a distance, horrified at what it looks like: "Oh, but it is dirty!" is the first line. The speaker, probably a woman, notes that this is a "little" filling station, "oil-soaked, oil-permeated," sounding worried, as if *she* will be the one required to scrub out the petroleum stains with their "over-all black translucency."

In the second stanza, the speaker zooms in on the human scene, noting that the station is family run, as "Father wears a dirty,/oil-soaked monkey suit" and "several quick and saucy/and greasy sons assist him" in running the family business.

Seeing the individuals, the speaker begins to change her tune, to ask human questions about the place such as "Do they live in the station?" Does the "dirty dog" on the greasy wicker furniture suggest family life?

In the fourth stanza, more domestic details emerge, as if the speaker is like a photographer with a zoom lens. We see "Some comic books," "a big dim doily" and a "big hirsute begonia." The "little" station of the first stanza is growing rapidly! The black and white of the earlier stanzas is gradually being filled in with color and texture. The "hirsute" or hairy begonia is almost human in its itchy skin.

The fifth stanza is filled with questions:

Why the extraneous plant?
Why the taboret?
Why, oh why, the doily?
(Embroidered in daisy stitch
with marguerites, I think,
and heavy with gray crochet.)

The details, especially of the embroidery, imply that the speaker, no longer distant, has zoomed right up close, so close she can count the stitches on the doily, examine the crochet border. She is no longer in her car; she has entered the space, and the closeness provides a new worldview and answers to her questions:

Somebody embroidered the doily,
Somebody waters the plant,
. . .
Somebody loves us all.

This poem is about America. Beginning with the image of the filling station seen at a distance, the poem presents us with the outsider's view of the place: dirty, worn, gray, taken over by technology ("high-strung automobiles") and hopelessness. But, as the speaker moves in closer, the scene takes on color and human form. Family emerges, first in the visible father and sons, and, in a more subtle way, the invisible mark of the women folk, the embroidery, and the flowers. The speaker, once cynical and unseeing, learns to see more carefully and to interpret what she sees. The new vision is a small epiphany: somebody loves us all!

In the modern America of Edsel failures and Pinto disasters, "Filling Station" is not a nostalgic poem. It is a joyous personal expression of faith in human nature to survive the blackest oil pollution. Even if the doily is gray and dingy, the carefully stitched daisies are in bloom.

Analytical   This is a more commonly required type of essay. Here, you are asked to analyze, or closely examine, some aspect of the story or poem or play. What are the particular literary techniques the writer has used, such as metaphors or similes? What themes emerge in the text? The sample essay is an analysis of Theodore Roethke's poem, "My Papa's Waltz."

Sample Essay: Analytical

Theodore Roethke's poem, "My Papa's Waltz," shows that even the most difficult parent is the object of a child's love. By careful use of point of view, Roethke presents a scene from childhood as a drunken father comes home to an angry wife and a loving child. Careful analysis of the language reveals that Roethke gives us the scene not exactly as the child sees it at the time, but as he, now grown up, remembers it.

The point of view is announced in the title, when the word "papa" is used instead of "father." This informal word alerts us that the language is that of a person familiar with the subject.

In the first stanza, we are abruptly presented with the problem:

The whiskey on your breath
Could make a small boy dizzy;

We immediately share the speaker's dilemma of meeting the drunken father as he comes home. The next two lines of the stanza prevent us from fearing harm as we learn of the speaker's determination to hang on "like death" as his father picks him up and dances around the kitchen with him. "Such waltzing was not easy" can be taken in the literal sense, it was hard to hang on, and in the metaphoric sense, that "such waltzing," that is, such a situation, was "not easy."

In the second stanza, we meet the other grown up, the mother, who, in the child's view, "Could not unfrown" herself, as she watches her drunken husband cavorting "until the pans/Slid from the kitchen shelf." The mother, however, is seen only at a distance. The child's concern, his memory, is of the father, whose presence is so special: even if he is drunk he provides a good time. The mother's inability to "unfrown" her face suggests she has seen such behavior before and no longer finds it amusing.

The third stanza introduces a hint of violence, revealing the father's hand "battered on one knuckle" and the boy, pressed so hard against his father's body that "every step you missed/My ear scraped on a buckle." These small details, the battered knuckle, the iron buckle, imply a tough father, prone to fighting, for whom even the pleasure of a game with his son carries a threat of danger, of pain.

In the last stanza, the boy is carried off to bed by his father. We learn more through the seemingly simple observations of the speaker; the father's hand is "caked with dirt," suggesting he is a working-class father who makes his money by manual labor. Like the bruise and the buckle of the previous stanza, the word "beat" can refer to the waltz rhythm, but also carries a suggestion of violence, as if the son might be beaten at any moment if the play turns to anger. The last line is powerful, implying that for all the fear and violence, the son loves his father. As he is waltzed off to bed he is "Still clinging" to his papa's shirt.

The language when we first read "My Papa's Waltz" seems simple and direct, as if the child is really telling it as it happens. Upon rereading, however, we realize how compact and loaded with meaning the images are, suggesting that far from being spontaneous, they are thoughtfully being reconstructed by a much older son who is remembering his father from a distance. The last line tells us, most of all, that even at this distance, he is "clinging," if not to the shirt, then to the recollection of a father who may have been rough, but was, after all, the only father he had.

Comparative   The comparative essay selects at least two works of literature, and begins with a thesis that shows a relationship between them. The body of the essay compares and contrasts the two (or more) works on the basis of three or four key points that are set out in the thesis. For instance, a student compares "Girl" and Gloria Naylor's "Kiswana Browne" on the basis of what they say about mother-daughter relationships. The student looks for similarities and also differences in the two works.

Sample Essay: Comparative

The relationship between mothers and daughters is a recurrent theme in stories by women, particularly African-American women writers in the twentieth century. For Gloria Naylor and Jamaica Kincaid, description of domestic life serves as a kind of code language for showing how two very different pairs of women come to terms with who they are, and how much they love one another.

Naylor's story "Kiswana Browne" is about a young woman who has changed her middle-class name of Melanie to Kiswana, and is trying to find her identity by moving into her own apartment in a run-down section of town not too far from the well-to-do suburb of Linden Hills where her mother still lives. One day, Kiswana looks out the window and sees her mother about to arrive for an unannounced visit. Her first reaction is shock: " 'Oh, God, it's Mama' " she exclaims. The daughter's mind immediately turns to the domestic details of the apartment, which her mother has never seen before. First, she "gave silent thanks that the elevator was broken" because this gives her a few extra minutes to clean up. As she races around putting things away, we learn something about her lifestyle: "She rushed to the sofa bed and hastily closed it without smoothing the rumpled sheets and blanket or removing her nightgown. She felt that somehow the tangled bedcovers would give away the fact that she had not slept alone last night." From this bit of detail, we can see that Kiswana, alias Melanie, feels guilty about having an affair with Abshu, and feels she has to hide the evidence of her activity from her mother. She continues to scurry around: "She took up his shaving cream and razor and threw them into the bottom drawer of her dresser beside her diaphragm. Mama wouldn't dare pry into my drawers right in front of me, she thought as she slammed the drawer shut. Well, at least not the *bottom* drawer. She may come up with some sham excuse for opening the top drawer, but never the bottom one."

Through these homey details, Naylor lets us learn a lot about Kiswana's rebellion from her middle-class parents. We learn that she has a lover with an African name, just as she has changed her own name to create a new identity. She is sleeping with him in her own apartment, trying to make it without help from her parents, even though this means living in a shabby building without much furniture. Her reaction to the sight of her mother, as revealed in the details of the dresser drawer, the tangled sheets, the shaving cream and the diaphragm, however, tells us that Kiswana is still a little bit afraid of her mother. Since she thinks her mother might still peek into the top drawer of the dresser, it seems as if she is saying that her mother still has control over her. Toward the end of the story, after she and her mother have had a long argument about politics, Kiswana "closed the door and turned around" and "spotted an envelope sticking between the cushions of her couch." Her mother has slipped her seventy-five much needed dollars. Kiswana is about to call out to her mother, but instead she changes her mind and "sat down in the chair with a long sigh . . . ." Just as she had hidden the diaphragm, her mother has hidden the envelope. In claiming it, and not calling her mother back, Kiswana demonstrates that she and her mother, for all their differences, are linked. Neither character says so directly, but the drawers and sheets and couch cushions tell the feelings in their own way, like a secret language between the two of them.

Similarly, Kincaid's story "Girl" uses domestic details to show another relationship between a mother and a daughter. Unlike Naylor's women, however, who are in a city, Kincaid's pair is in a rural setting. Instead of seeing events through the eyes of the daughter, this time we see them mostly from the mother's point of view. Kincaid's story does not use the third-person narrative Naylor's does, but is told in an unusual second-person voice. "Wash the white clothes on Monday" the story begins, and the reader has to figure out for herself what is going on. "Cook pumpkin fritters in very hot sweet oil;

soak your little cloths right after you take them off . . . ." At first it all seems a jumble. We find, however, that like Naylor, Kincaid is piling up domestic details and asking us to think about them as we figure out that the narrator is a mother speaking to her daughter: "this is how to sew on a button; this is how to make a buttonhole for the button you have just sewed on; this is how to hem a dress when you see the hem coming down and so to prevent yourself from looking like the slut I know you are so bent on becoming . . . ."

It is at the word "slut" that we realize there is something about this mother-daughter relationship that reminds us of Kiswana and her mother. It's as if, in the little girl, we have Kiswana at a young age, and in the mother instructing her daughter, a reflection of the younger Mrs. Browne. "Slut" is a powerful word, suggesting according to the *Oxford English Dictionary*, "a woman of low or loose character." The sewing on of the button, like all of the other domestic duties, is provided almost as if to stop the girl from growing up to be a "slut," as the mother might see Kiswana later on. The domestic chores are supposed to keep the girl busy and out of trouble.

If the two stories are different in these ways, they share a common theme nevertheless. In the end, Kiswana's mother tucks the envelope between the sofa cushions; the girl's mother ends by saying, "you mean to say that after all you are really going to be the kind of woman who the baker won't let near the bread?" Clearly, both mothers are proud of their daughters, even if they cannot say so directly. The envelope to help pay the rent supports Kiswana's move toward independence, and perhaps makes her feel silly about the bottom drawer. The girl's mother's reference to the baker makes clear that she, too, wants a daughter who can stand up for herself and assert her independence. Both mothers, through their domestic language, overcome the generation gap and express love and understanding for their daughters.

Argumentative   This essay aims to persuade the reader to share your opinion or interpretation of the literary work. The sample essay on Randall Jarrell's "The Death of the Ball Turret Gunner" and Wilfred Owen's "Dulce et Decorum Est" argues for the inhumanity of war.

Sample Essay: Argumentative

Wilfred Owen died in 1918, just as World War I ended; Randall Jarrell was born in 1914, just as the war that killed Owen had begun. Both are poets who argue eloquently against simplistic ideas of patriotism. Randall Jarrell's poem, "The Death of the Ball Turret Gunner" is only five lines long, but it presents one of the most impassioned antiwar statements of modern times. When we read it alongside Wilfred Owen's "Dulce et Decorum Est," a poem written in the first world war, we can only conclude that even the best poets are helpless when it comes to stopping the insanity of war.

"Dulce et Decorum Est" argues through powerful sensual images to persuade the folks back home not to accept propagandist descriptions of what it was like to be a soldier on the front lines. Owen uses irony to get his point across, especially with his title. "Dulce et Decorum Est" comes from a Latin poet and means "It is sweet and fitting." The rest of the line comes at the end of the poem, "to die for one's country." At the beginning of the poem, the reader might assume the speaker is taking the expected patriotic stance, as Horace did, arguing for the necessity of war. By the end of the poem, we are persuaded otherwise. Each section of the poem focuses our attention on one of the five senses, so that we experience the war in all its brutality. We *see* the horror of men "Bent double, like old beggars under sacks/Knock-kneed" as they march asleep on their feet. "Many had lost their boots/But limped on, blood-shod." They are "lame" and "blind," so that while we can see them, they can no longer see. Later, the speaker tells us that "In all my dreams before my helpless sight" he continues to *see* the horrors of a gas attack. "Gas! GAS! Quick, boys!" someone calls, and new senses are introduced as we seem to smell the green, poison gas that chokes the man unable to get his gas mask on in time. As he dies, the speaker hears "the blood/Come gurgling from the froth-corrupted lungs" as the body is tossed into a wagon. Owen uses a simile to try to describe the desperate acts of the man who is gassed: "flound'ring like a man in fire or lime" because he knows his audience, as nonsoldiers, cannot *see* the real event. Finally, after all the images are piled up like the dead bodies in the cart, he concludes his argument:

> My friend, you would not tell with such high zest
> To children ardent for some desperate glory,
> The old lie: *Dulce et decorum est*
> *Pro Patria mori.*

In Randall Jarrell's poem, the "if" isn't even possible. There seems to be no hope, only the inevitable inhumane bureaucratic death by war. The short poem is worth quoting in full:

> From my mother's sleep I fell into the State.
> And I hunched in its belly till my wet fur froze.
> Six miles from earth, loosed from its dream of life,
> I woke to black flak and the nightmare fighters.
> When I died they washed me out of the turret with a hose.

In Owen's poem, at least we still recognized real men at war; they were men who recognized horror, had nightmares, and felt the loss of their comrades. What is so scary about Jarrell's image is that it conjures up the aloneness of the gunner. He is barely human, no longer a comrade in arms, but a mere animal, a creature no sooner born, his "fur" still "wet," than he is plunged into use by the State as a gunner. If Owen uses irony, so does Jarrell, but it is a colder, harsher irony, as the point of view twists in the last line, and the gunner describes his own end: "When I died they washed me out of the turret with a hose." Thus he speaks not only for himself, but for all those silenced by the bureaucracy and madness of war. Just as Owen's narrator tells the story of his lost comrades, so the narrator here tells a similar tale, but, ironically, it is his story as well as theirs. The brevity of the poem is like the quick, short life of the young recruit, no sooner born than he is old enough to enlist, and die.

Both poems argue powerfully, through their images and their ironic tone, against war. If the world is still fighting wars it can only mean that politicians just don't read enough poetry.

WRITING THE FIRST DRAFT

Once you have limited the topic, and figured out which strategy is best for the ideas you want to express, you can write the first draft. The first draft is not just an outline. It is an attempt at a full, complete essay, meant to be read by someone else. Write the thesis statement first, as part of the introductory paragraph. Then plan your body paragraphs. A 500-word essay might have a total of five paragraphs, so you'll be writing an introduction (with a thesis), three body paragraphs, and a conclusion. Look closely at the sample essays to see how the writer decided when to start a new paragraph. Look at the use of transitions to start new paragraphs as well. Select the quotes from the works of literature you are using that will support your argument. Each body paragraph should have at least one quotation from the work of literature you are discussing.

Type your draft, double spaced, using the manuscript guidelines provided by your instructor for the final copy. If your instructor allows a handwritten draft, use ink, and double space, leaving wide margins. This will make revision much easier. After you write the first draft, try to get some feedback. Your instructor may read the draft and offer suggestions for revision. In addition, you can exchange drafts with a classmate and offer each other suggestions. Ask the reader if your thesis is clear and whether you have enough quotes to support the thesis.

REVISING

After you receive some suggestions, revise the essay. Think of this as "revision," that is, seeing the essay again. A good revision requires:

rewriting the thesis to make it clearer

checking that there are clear transitions between paragraphs

checking that all quotations are copied correctly

making any necessary corrections for spelling, grammar, and sentence structure

Once you have rethought and rewritten your draft, you are ready to create the final copy of the manuscript. When you submit a manuscript, you must make it look neat and professional. Follow these guidelines:

1. Cover Page

Each essay should have a cover or title page. Center the title of the essay in the middle of the page. About two-thirds down, list:

your full name

your student identification number

the professor's name

the course code number

the assignment number

the date

2. Manuscript Pages

All pages are typed and double spaced.

Each page is numbered and headed with your last name in front of the page number.

Leave wide margins: 1 1/2 inch on the left, and 1 inch at the top, bottom, and right-hand side.

Titles of novels, plays, books and any long work of literature (like the epic *Paradise Lost*) must be underlined. Short pieces—poems, short stories—are put in quotation marks each time they are used in the essay, for example, "Filling Station."

If your instructor requires it, be sure you have included a citation with the page on which the quote appears each time you quote from a poem, play, or story in the text. Put the page number in parentheses after the quotation.

If you have any questions about manuscript format, ask your instructor.

RESPONDING TO COMMENTS

When your instructor has read your essay, he/she will return it to you with comments. You should rewrite the essay, using the comments as guidelines for revision. As you plan the revision, pay attention to:

- Thesis: Is the thesis clear, and does the essay support and prove the thesis in the body paragraphs?
- Organization: Are the paragraphs planned carefully, with clear and effective transitions?
- Use of quotations: Did you quote enough/too much?
- Writing errors: Are spelling, grammar, sentence structure, and mechanics correct?

After you review the manuscript, you may resubmit it to the instructor. You may also share your revision with classmates to see if the comments have been responded to adequately.

PART TWO

The Elements of Literature

CHAPTER 3

Writing about Fiction

Writing about fiction is your chance to enter a house that from the outside looks forbiddingly large and mysterious. But having entered, you find many interesting and delightfully arranged rooms filled with sunlight to explore, all really yours alone to enjoy, examine, and describe.

Although the instructor may review for you formal literary criticism (a large, well-appointed room with great oak beams and stained-glass windows), the points to be covered in your paper should reflect your thoughts and feelings about the literary work at hand.

Think of fiction at the outset of our discussion as a counterfeiting, a making up and manipulation of a series of events and characters and their thoughts. We first encountered fiction as children when we read or had read to us the classic stories assigned to children from Grimm's *Fairy Tales*, Aesop's *Fables*, and other similar works. Children's fiction, whether classic or contemporary, does not completely help us to understand fiction, but it does indicate that we are familiar with it.

As you write about fiction, you should next ask yourself if you like or dislike the work you read and why. Did you like what happened and the way it happened? In addition, you might consider the possibility that other readers liked the work as much as you did. Why would this be so? What elements of a Chekhov story could be as important to you as to a student in Russia or India or France? Which elements in Dickens' novels have made them so universally acclaimed? You may be intrigued by the plot, the events that lead you deeper and deeper into the story. You may share the same emotions as a character, and would do the same thing he or she would do in similar situations. You may have discovered yourself enveloped in a certain mood as you read. Was that an accident?

Great fiction resonates with universal human experience. The rules of human conduct tend to be informally agreed on in many diverse cultures, including primitive ones even before there were ten commandments. Earlier peoples had been inclined to behave morally before such conduct became codified by law. The writer often reflects what is already deeply rooted in humankind. It may be these abiding universal truths that make us like a work of fiction.

As you know from the first chapter, there are several schools of literary criticism, some old, some new. Authors, however, rarely write to the beat of such criticism; they are assigned to a particular school after the fact. They may write at a specific time and be influenced by the style and events of that period. However, writers such as Nathaniel Hawthorne, James Joyce, Franz Kafka, Richard Wright, and Flannery O'Connor were innovators of narrative styles, and found ways to write that differed from those of writers who came before them.

Consequently, you'd do well to think of the uniqueness of the writer before you write about the work. When did the author live and where? What was going on at the time that the writer *may* have been influenced by? Where did the writer travel and what happened when she or he got there? What kind of work did the writer do in addition to writing? (Many writers have held a variety of jobs before and while writing; several of them were journalists like Hemingway or physicians like Chekhov.) What books did the writer read? What unusual experiences, if any, did the writer have? Consider that the writer, like those cited above, discovered something new to write about or a new way of writing about something often written before, some aspect of characterization or narrative that illustrates an unusual perception of the human condition.

Remember that the blank page for the writer is like a new world about to be discovered—just as it is for you. You and the writer are heirs to the oldest means of communication exclusive of voice sounds and hand signs. (The telephone is only 125 years old; television is barely 65.) In the life of humankind writing itself is a relatively recent means of making communications visible— perhaps something over 7,500 years old. And at the very start of this literary history there was fiction. The Egyptian *Tales of the Magicians,* a collection of stories from about 4000 B.C., naturally supposes even earlier beginnings. Other narrative works have come from India, ancient Israel, the kingdoms of the Euphrates, the Greeks, the Arabs, and from many other peoples and places.

The creative urge to tell stories is universally one of the strongest emotions in human beings. Fiction, of course, is not all pure creation; sometimes it is the reworking of experience or communal history—that is, making reality fit fictional needs which then often go beyond reality to make specific points. Our earliest fiction consisted of moral writing; good things happened to good people (or animals) and bad things happened to bad people (or animals). Perhaps this is as it should be, but it is not what most of us understand about reality today. The drive to write fiction that in part or whole is didactic (morally instructive) is still obvious in the work of many contemporary writers of fiction.

Writing about fiction should be something of both challenge and opportunity, exploration and discovery. What does *this* writer have to say—and how does he or she say it? you might ask yourself. A story or a novel is a special room in the house you are visiting. Unlike television where you see the story, fiction makes you envision it, stretch your knowledge and imagination to match the author's. Understand, though, that most writers *are* writers because writing is for them the most lasting, perhaps even the most natural way they can reach out to others. "Writing," of course, is a combination of thinking *and* writing, as we shall see.

THE ELEMENTS OF FICTION

Once you sense the uniqueness of an author and the significance of his or her work, you should be able to write critically about it. Critical writing requires you to deal with key elements of fiction. These elements are discussed in the section that follows.

Plot

Plot is the arrangement of related events, however simple or complex, in the narrative of a work of fiction with the result that subsequently some conflict around which the story revolves will be concluded. (All fiction does not contain the same degree of conflict, and there is fiction in which there is very little conflict.) Plotting a story is the ordering of a world and the lives of the characters who inhabit it. William Faulkner wrote: "I like to think of the world I created as being a kind of keystone in the universe; that small as the keystone is, if it were ever taken away the universe itself would collapse."

The real world is rarely within our ability to control. But fiction offers a "splendid economy" an artistic ordering to counteract what Henry James' observation that life is splendid waste, "all is conclusion and confusion."

Aristotle in his *Poetics* calls plot the first element of drama or epic, which is composed of three elements. (1) a beginning that presumes additional action, (2) a middle that considers previous action and presumes succeeding action, and (3) an end that requires attention to earlier events but anticipates no further action.

Over the years Aristotle's three elements have been increased to five, more clearly defined fundamentals of plot. They are: (1) the beginning and exposition which set the plot (or plots) in motion; (2) rising action, a series of actions, each of which causes another to begin and which considers the importance of tension and conflict (earlier critics used "conflict" and "crisis" interchangeably); (3) the climax, the most critical section of the narrative; (4) falling action, a lessening of tension, during which time some degree of tension (or suspension) is still maintained together with the explanation of the related events, sometimes called the denouement; (5) the resolution of the conflict—the happy or unhappy ending.

Whether you prefer the pure Aristotelian formula for plot or its expanded contemporary version, remember that plot in fiction is the structuring or ordering of the narrative. How does Kate Chopin plot a story in a brief moment of time, while Kafka seems to embrace all of time in a story like "A Hunger Artist"? How does any writer create and heighten conflict and how is it resolved? Why does Leslie Marmon Silko divide "The Man to Send Rain Clouds" into sections? And does Arna Bontemps' "A Summer Tragedy" conform to Aristotle's definition of plot? These are some of the questions you might want to consider as you write about fiction. (Plot is in the map room of the house.)

Character

The people you come to know in stories or novels are characters; they create action in the narrative. They tend to be the focus of the work. John Dryden believed that "the story is the least part" of a work, the character the most important. The writer creates the characters and supplies us with the information that allows us to identify, positively or negatively, with them. We know something about how the characters look, live, and think; often we know about their jobs and their social status, their aspirations and problems. We enter their heads—as we cannot with real people in real life—and share their emotions; we have access to the most secret and intimate corridors of their being. It is here where character motivation originates and plot commences. If the writer has done well, the character is revealed to the reader, act by act, spoken word by spoken word, thought by thought, like a flower unfolding petal by petal in the summer sun.

Not infrequently you will find characters so strongly drawn that they become the titles of the works they are in, for example, Charles Dickens' *Martin Chuzzlewit*, or Henry James' *Daisy Miller*, or Herman Melville's *Billy Budd*, Sailor: *An Inside Narrative*, or Stephen Crane's *Maggie: A Girl of the Streets*. Short stories like Hawthorne's "Young Goodman Brown" and Gloria Naylor's "Kiswana Browne" indicate the continuing popularity of character titles involving people of all kinds of stations who function as fictional heroes and heroines.

Good characters must have dimension—that is, not merely inhabit the narrative for the sake of being there. The character must function; plot must turn on the character's actions; dialogue between characters must move plot as well as enlarge the character. It is crucial that we know everything about a character that is pertinent to the story, and perhaps that knowledge will resonate beyond the bounds of fiction. For example, we *want* to know what happens to the hero and heroine in "The Lady with the Pet Dog," for we invest in them as people and wonder about their destinies. That is what good writing and vivid characterization do. (Character can be found in the screening room.)

Point of View

Point of view is the position in which the writer places the character, around whom move all the elements of fiction. Point of view, like the defined area seen through a camera lens, is the frame or boundary of a work of fiction. Frequently it is through the point of view that we discover different ways of telling a story.

Traditionally there are three basic points of view: the first person or "I"; the somewhat experimental second person or "you"; and the third person "he," "she," "it," or "they."

First-person point of view is the method by which the author centrally positions one person through whom the story is told. Every detail of the work is filtered through that character who cannot intimately know others; he or she is the "I" character of the first-person singular. This is a limiting, but often effective way of writing, but that may be precisely what the author desires. This might be called a high-intensity point of view, providing the author with a special and perhaps unique voice in a strictly circumscribed world. Joyce's "Araby" and Louise Erdrich's "Snares" are two examples of the use of the internal or "I" voice.

Daniel Defoe's *Robinson Crusoe,* Joseph Conrad's *Lord Jim,* and Herman Melville's *Moby Dick* are but three of many novels in which writers have used the first-person voice effectively. The first-person point of view dictates that the protagonist can examine himself inside out, but most constantly decipher the acts and words of others to examine himself. (Untraditionally, however, there can be more than one "I" character in the same work. For example, if there are three people at the scene of a crime—the perpetrator, the victim, and a witness—the crime can be related by each character in turn, therefore bringing different first-person points of view to the story.)

The use of the third-person or external voice gives writers far more leeway—though they may not use it. The "I" becomes "he" or "she" and this lets the writer use the *limited* or *pseudo* third person, focusing not on several characters, but one, as in Wright's "The Man Who Was Almost a Man." From this point of view, the writer moves that character from a distance, and does not become one with the "I." No other character is really penetrated, or certainly not to the degree the protagonist has been. Sometimes, as in Bontemps' "A Summer Tragedy," two characters, Jennie and Jeff Patton, can become the third person of a story. Third person can be compared to a camera that has been focused between closeup and wide-angle, and it is this point of view many authors use to make us see a resemblance between fiction and the real world. The interior experiences of a singular major character are such that we can readily share them. Nothing stands between the writer and reader but the manipulated distance provided by the third person. Gone is the intrusive authorial voice of past use of the point of view (often opinionated, or editorializing and addressing the reader directly by the pronoun "you"). In modern fiction the characters speak; no authors are allowed.

Readers tend to identify more readily with one major character, though they seem to prefer the larger reality offered by the third-person voice over the first-person. Both, however, are widely used in the short story.

Unlimited third-person and omniscient or objective points of view are essentially the same. Herein, the author views all characters from an equal, objective stance; she can enter all their minds or none; the writer can share knowledge of one or more characters with every other character in the work. With the omniscient or unlimited third person and a large number of characters, through the use of the *interior monologue,* much like the dramatic soliloquy, the author can let us know how much one character knows about another. This achieves dynamic progress in the same way film is used to create anticipation and tension through montage. But sacrificed by this point of view is the sense of closeness to character found in the first person or limited third person. Here the author is truly a god, aiming characters at each other, constructing plots, establishing settings, issuing subjects and themes couched in a variety of styles, all conveyed through a team of characters.

Leo Tolstoy's *War and Peace* is a great model for the use of the omniscient point of view. The novel is a vibrant animism that conveys the movements of people and history. Tolstoy uses more than 500 characters ranging from peasant to Napoleon, with the key players meeting or crossing paths at crucial times after earlier being introduced in alternating chapters. The distance between author and characters is not always equal, since the major actors are only three of the multitude: Natasha Rostova, Prince Andrei Bolkonski, and Pierre Bezukhov.

Shifts in point of view may be indicated by a new paragraph, a space break in the narrative, or nothing at all. E. M. Forster declared that with an effective shift of viewpoint the writer has the power "to bounce the reader into accepting what he says." Dickens' *Bleak House,* Stevenson's *Dr. Jekyll and Mr. Hyde,* as well as Tolstoy's epic, present examples of shifting points of view. Shifting points of view may come as relief to some readers, a change of pace. For the writer, they expand or contract perception, allow a closeup or telephoto angle.

Tense usage combined with point of view offers tempting avenues for experimentation. Present tense makes narrative seem as though events are occurring as you read them; past tense is more leisurely and is used with greater frequency. A writer might shift point of view between first person, third person, and omniscient for certain specific effects (closeness or distance) and at the same time shift from past to present tense for certain other effects, for instance, pacing—speeding or slowing down the action. Traditionally, however, fiction is usually presented in only one tense and one point of view.

Setting

Setting is the physical place and time where action occurs in a narrative. Place and time are of immense importance in establishing the mood of a work of fiction.

Just as characters often are the titles of novels and stories they are in, places, too, are frequently titles—for example, Langston Hughes' "On the Road," Eudora Welty's "A Worn Path," and Ernest Hemingway's "A Clean, Well-Lighted Place." In Welty's "A Worn Path," for example, an elderly black woman wills her aching body across fields and woods to secure medicine for her sick grandchild. Welty's setting, rich in imagery and symbolism, grows to almost epic proportions, an odyssey of sorts, expressing the greatness of the human spirit.

We feel a sense of comfort with the familiar. When we read a book whose settings are known to us, or see a film set in a city that we either live in or have visited, we feel closer to the story. Yet, we are also curious about places and times we know little about. Edgar Allan Poe's "The Masque of the Red

Death," considered one of his greatest stories, has a setting that is as much in Prince Prospero's mind as it is in the castle to which he retires to escape the plague. We are drawn into the story to ricochet between the "real" and another level of imagination, terror.

As we know, a setting in fiction is not fixed as in many plays—is not real, but a construction of words designed to give the reader a sense of place through description. But settings can also be deceptive. Shirley Jackson's "The Lottery" begins in a small American town (like the one in "Young Goodman Brown" quite possibly) on a day that is "clear and sunny," but ends with a character screaming, "It isn't fair, it isn't right." (Jackson, like Poe, is a fine writer of Gothic horror.)

Settings can be physical as well as symbolic, as Welty's title suggests. In short, setting is where the fiction lives.

Tone

Tone, which we also find in poetry and drama, is the "attitude" of the author in a work of fiction. When we speak of a story as being happy or sad, comic or tragic, ironic or satiric, we are trying to establish the writer's attitude toward his or her materials. Sometimes it is easy to establish the tone of a story. For example, the very title of Arna Bontemps' "A Summer Tragedy" indicates the author's perspective on the action. At other times, we have a sudden shift in tone that turns the title into an ironic commentary. Tone can also be a complex subject, embracing matters of setting and mood, characterization, narrative action, and style. Consider Amy Tan's story "Two Kinds." The story presents a young, somewhat rebellious girl who knows she doesn't have the talents her mother ascribes to her. Yet, there are moments when, briefly, she thinks she does. Then comes the moment when she deliberately—though this might not altogether be the case—performs badly enough to make her mother have doubts. As behavior shifts, the tone also shifts from small hope to failure and to guilt because Jing-mei has failed to keep alive the immigrant's dream of becoming "anything you wanted to be in America." The "voice" changes, becomes more reflective and mellow when Jing-mei reaches thirty and looks back on her childhood. Moreover, there is another voice in the story, the mother's, which lends tension to the story, heightens the conflict between mother and daughter and between reality and possibility. Here the tone is at first hopeful, then desperate, and finally, defeated. The reconciliation when Jing-mei is an adult is sad and touching, and this is the final tonality in an admittedly complex tale.

Symbolism

A symbol is a representation of a reality on one level that has a corresponding reality on another level; symbols are things that represent other things by habit, association, or convention. Symbols in fiction, poetry, and drama possess specific points of reference created by the writer to lead you to and inside the work. *Symbols* are most often associated with *allegory* (Greek: "to speak other"). Allegory has two levels of meaning, but the second meaning is to be read beneath and concurrent with the surface story and may well itself be an extended story. In Kay Boyle's "The Astronomer's Wife," symbolism and allegory are relatively easy to discern. You may wish to discuss the symbolism expressed by the occupations of Mrs. Ames' husband and the plumber, or the allegory that further describes *where* they work, or the similarities between a plumber's pipe and an astronomer's telescope. In Franz Kafka's "A Hunger Artist," a more complex story, you can find several meanings that can be read as ironic or tragic, as well as allegorical. Edgar Allan Poe's "The Masque of the Red Death" abounds in allegory. A critical reading of these works should help you understand the various levels of meaning they contain.

Style

Style is found in the way a work of fiction is written. George Henry Lewes, who lived with Marian Evans (whose pen name was George Eliot), listed five rules of style: (1) economy (conciseness with precision); (2) simplicity; (3) sequential development of plot; (4) the inevitability of climax; and (5) variety.

These rules seem to still be valid even though language has changed tremendously since Lewes' time. But modern applications also see style as the way certain rhythms are employed in fiction writing; the way authors choose their words and use abstract, concrete, and figurative language; and the way they handle all the traditional elements of fiction—plot, character, point of view, setting, and theme. These, too, have been modified by time, and as these have been altered, so too has the heading under which more recent works fall: post-modernism.

But for many writers style is simply the way they write, the way words occur to them while shaping their fiction. For others, style may have developed over time through studying, consciously or subconsciously, the work of still other writers.

Writers who have journalism backgrounds, like Hemingway or Martha Gellhorn, may write in a style quite different from the one used by writers who also write or have written poetry, like Robert Penn Warren. Few poets, Walt Whitman being one of the exceptions, emerge from a background in journalism. There are many factors that may help to shape a style. And of course there are writers without any writing background who love language and ultimately find themselves to be writers.

Hemingway, whose style a generation of writers tried to copy, is known for his Spartan prose which is almost devoid of adjectives and adverbs, and for his use of plain language. These helped to make him clearly understandable and accessible. Ford Madox Ford said, "Hemingway's words strike you, each one, as if they were pebbles fetched from a brook."

William Faulkner's style is rotund, full-blown, expansive, and not very accessible—which led Hemingway to say of him, "Poor Faulkner. Does he really think big emotions come from big words?"

But then critic Max Eastman said Hemingway had "a literary style . . . of wearing false hair on the chest." Both Faulkner and Hemingway are Nobel laureates in literature.

Theme

To some readers theme and subject mean the same thing. They are quite different. Matthew Arnold wrote that "all depends on subject: choose a fitting action, penetrate yourself with the feeling of its situations; this done, everything will follow."

Theme, however, really is the distillation of subject; it makes relevant all the words that are used to frame the theme, which is the fine print of subject. The following brief dialogue examines the difference between subject and theme.

STUDENT A: "What's the book about?"
STUDENT B: "War." [Subject]
STUDENT A: "War?"
STUDENT B: "Actually, the horrors experienced by soldiers at the Battle of the Bulge. [Theme]

The subject is general; the theme is a specific statement about the subject. The same principle might be applied to Tolstoy, who wrote about *armies* in *War and Peace* and Hemingway, whose writings included pieces on the *units* of armies in three wars. The poet Wilfred Owen once said, "My subject is War, and the pity of War. The poetry is in the pity." Owen thus defines the difference between subject and theme in his own work.

INTERPRETING FICTION

Your interpretation of a literary work begins with accepting its theme, its diction and construction, what the work conveys to you, and your reaction to it. You accept the writing as a complete entity, a work of art, that possesses values you and other readers respect.

That done, you will find it worthwhile to review the elements of fiction to see if they are present or mostly present in the story you are interpreting. Then it may be expedient to note the theme of the story. If we took Chekhov's "The Lady with the Pet Dog," would we be seeing another "star-crossed lovers" theme or quite some other theme?

You might try to describe the kind of man Gurov is and decide whether or not there is irony in how he has changed by the end of the story. How has his openness to the "encounters of life" contributed to the plot? How effective are plot and character in support of theme? Point of view? With the questions and your answers digested, you can then move to the author's motive, if any, for writing the story. Chekhov is very good at detail that is important to his stories, so it will help if you read this (or any other story) more than once.

There are not, really, as many kinds of fiction as there are poetry, but it would be unfair to poetry to say that it does not require as much analysis as fiction; the amount of analysis depends on the work under study, not because it is one genre or the other. Most stories, however, are longer than most poems, and will require longer, more analytical reading. Some poems provide clues to their meanings by the way they are structured on the page, with some lines indented, very brief stanzas, or the use of punctuation: colons, for instance, or dashes. In a poem, these clues tend to leap out.

Such is not the case with most fiction. Outward appearances on the printed page reveal nothing. Reading is the only way to dig out the elements necessary for you to write about fiction. A first reading of a story may reveal its plot and then its theme. Plots generally come to life first, but not the theme within, so it may take a second or third reading before theme emerges. Plot, as you know, is the element in fiction where tension and conflict are found.

Once you have a good idea of what the story is about you can gather the characters on stage to see how well they have carried and moved plot, if their motivations, inner thoughts, dialogues and actions support your possible conclusions about the theme. You will want to describe the function of each character as part of your analysis.

Anton Chekhov said, "Cut a good story anywhere and it will bleed." (He was a doctor, remember.) Would the story you're reading lose anything if it had not been written the way it is? Could you cross out a paragraph and still have the story make sense, or eliminate a character without disturbing the plot? Imagine Philip Roth's "The Conversion of the Jews" without the janitor, Yakov Blotnik; would the story still work? Is the protagonist, Ozzie Freedman, unreasonable? Can you find, subtly located, the reason for Ozzie's behavior, which explains the nature of the conflict? Crucial differences between Itzie and Ozzie arise early in the story. How do they become manifest at the climax of the story?

Notice the shifts in points of view. Do they help you to understand the story, and in which ways? How do the breaks in the story add to its tension? These are the kinds of questions you should ask yourself and find answers to in order to write cogently about any story.

Remember that interpretations of fiction are not engraved in stone. Unless an author tells us of her intention in writing the story, or what the theme most assuredly is, or why a character does this or says that, we simply cannot know for sure why a story is the way it is. We just examine what has been given to us and come to the best interpretation we can which is, as it can only be, your opinion.

EVALUATING FICTION

A famous painter said, "A painting is valuable to you if *you* like it." In the same light, a work of fiction is valuable to you if you appreciate it for what it is. But that is only the beginning. Almost none of us is comfortable being alone in an evaluative process.

Students of literature can take heart: There is a proven track record of great fiction, whether we agree with it or not. In any case, the record is always changing. Herman Melville may be on the record for a number of years, and then he is off it; the same with Henry James and Virginia Woolf. The record may showcase at a given time some of the great Russian writers—Dostoyevski, Chekhov, and Tolstoy, for example—but never cite Leonid Andreyev. Some astoundingly good writers have never been on the record, like Martha Gellhorn. It would be a serious mistake not to read the record for information and assistance.

The following questions can help to guide you in your evaluation of a story or novel:

- Is the plot predictable or original?
- Do the characters have unique and well-developed dimensions or are they simply flat or stock types?
- Is the setting strikingly conveyed or are time, place, and atmosphere underdeveloped?
- Does the symbolism, if present, enhance the story or does it merely seem tacked on or confusing?
- Is the theme provocative and consequential or relatively unimportant or trite?
- Is the author's use of language original or not at all memorable?
- Which critical approach seems most useful in evaluating this work of fiction, and why?

Great fiction engages the universe and millions of readers, each of whom relates to it differently, yet somehow the same. And that is the way we really are. Great fiction has the ability to draw us into it as individuals and as members of a community called humanity stuck in space. We can find knowledge and comfort in fiction, pride and sorrow. Fiction is, after all, merely a reflection of what we are, have been, and perhaps may be.

CHAPTER 4

Writing about Poetry

*E*xperts generally acknowledge poetry as the oldest form of literature, but the "problem of defining it is the problem of defining its extraordinariness," as one critic observes.

The earliest poetry we know is narrative poetry, which reflected the history, celebrations, beliefs, and mores of ancient peoples in the Egyptian offering lists, utterances, and papyri; in the Greek epics, the Indian Vedas, the Norse sagas, the Hebrew Old Testament, the Babylonian Gilgamesh epic, and elsewhere. Robert Graves called these narratives a "dramatic shorthand record." Cicero believed that the poet performed invaluable service by recording the deeds of national heroes and noble men. What poetry *is* and what it *does* are questions that have been debated for centuries.

Matthew Arnold said, "There are two offices of poetry—one to add to one's store of thoughts and feelings—another to compose and elevate the mind by sustained tone, numerous allusions, and a grand style." Arnold's is a late definition of poetry which for centuries had been considered a kind of *fiction,* wherein stories were told and a "faigning" (feigning) observable. Sir Philip Sidney thought poetry was "distinctive" because it joined philosophy and history, a theory that John Donne also believed. William Wordsworth in his Preface saw the debate about what poetry is as one concerned with the differences between "matter of fact and science." He was joined in this opinion by Samuel Taylor Coleridge and Leigh Hunt. There is for all discussion, however, one monumental difference today between poetry and prose, and it is that prose mimics ordinary speech, while poetic language is extraordinary in the selection of words it uses and in its metrical rhythms. A stanza from Donne's sardonic "Song" (Go and Catch a Falling Star) provides an example of unusual language filled with bite and imagery:

> Go and catch a falling star
>> Get with child a mandrake root,
> Tell me where all past years are,
>> Or who cleft the Devil's foot,

Teach me to hear mermaids singing,
Or to keep off envy's stinging,
      And find
      What wind
Serves to advance an honest mind.

In this single stanza we find stated divisions between "matter of fact" and science, and myth and personal observation. (Donne, after a rakish youth, became a clergyman.) Prose, it was believed by the leading Romantic writers, was better suited for scientific exposition than poetry. Thomas Mann insisted that it was "a fruitless and futile mania" for critics to keep probing for differences between the works of prose writers and poets. Ezra Pound agreed, saying that "all essays about 'poetry' are usually not only dull but inaccurate" and without value.

Poetry is further distinguished by structure or form and its use of meter, which produces rhythm and rhyme. Conversely, some poetry relies heavily on imagery and very little on rhythm and rhyme. In sum, the now traditional differences between poetry and prose are these: poetry *may* be written in meter, but prose is not; poetry *may* use rhyme, while prose does not; poetry most often uses "a special language," but, for the most part, prose does not. (Joyce, of course, would be one of several exceptions.)

The major characteristic of poetry as it evolved through the ages has become its ability to distill monumental themes down to their essences. (We rarely today see a poem that fills a book, like *The Iliad* or *The Odyssey*.) In a time when Americans are said to be upset by global politics, the following two poems might be considered not only prophetic, but good examples of the distillation of themes that have always concerned us. The first, "America" by Claude McKay, is in traditional, fourteen-line, iambic pentameter, sonnet form. The second, by e. e. cummings, "next to of course god," is in "open" or "free verse" form. Consider not only the topic, but the differences in structure, language, and tone:

Although she feeds me bread of bitterness,
And sinks into my throat her tiger's tooth,
Stealing my breath of life, I will confess
I love this cultured hell that tests my youth!
Her vigor flows like tides into my blood,
Giving me strength against her hate.
Her bigness sweeps my being like a flood.
Yet as a rebel fronts a kind in state,
I stand within her walls with not a shred
Of terror, malice, not a word of jeer.
Darkly I gaze into the days ahead,
And see her might and granite wonders there,
Beneath the touch of Time's unerring hand,
Like priceless treasures sinking in the sand.

                        ●   ●   ●

"next to of course god america i
love you land of the pilgrims' and so forth oh

say can you see by the dawn's early my
country 'tis of centuries come and go
and are no more what of it we should worry
in every language even deafanddumb
thy sons acclaim your glorious name by gorry
by jingo by gee by gosh by gum
why talk of beauty what could be more beautiful
than these heroic happy dead
who rushed like lions to the roaring slaughter
they did not stop to think they died instead
then shall the voice of liberty be mute."

He spoke. And drank rapidly a glass of water.

A single reading of a poem, short or long, is not enough to perceive its meaning, for a poem is somewhat like a mystery to be solved, or a language to be understood. Poetry should be studied line by line. Because of its nature to compress or distill, every word in a poem tends to bear more weight than every word in a story or novel. "Sound out" a poem; read it aloud to detect what silent readings may not offer up. Better still, go to poetry readings remembering that poems were originally *sung* and that there are still places in the world where poets and sometimes musical instruments are called singers.

It is important to know when, approximately, a poem was written; as suggested in the fiction section, it is also helpful to know something about the author and his or her life. A poem's title may also give you a clue as to its theme, and with each reading you'll discover more about the work and find yourself responding to it. That's what the poet wants; that's what any writer wants, because the crucial importance about a poem is that you, the reader, come to feel what the poet wants you to. If this occurs, that means you have penetrated his or her imaginative arena, unlocked the mystery, understood the language.

Poets, being "the athletes of language," according to Robert Boynton, are forever challenging our ability to keep up with them. They are like drummers in the band called Literature: they set the pace, diminish or augment it with new or different chords, "sound," images, signals. If we as players somehow lose the beat, we need only "listen" closely to the drummer to get back to it. Poetry is not confined to books; folk singers, blues singers, rockers, and rappers are "the poets of everyday," their lyrics perhaps more current, but certainly linked to the way many people have thought and felt over time.

Your understanding of and sensitivities about popular music may help you with the study of poetry and strengthen the confidence you have in your ability to understand, enjoy, and write about poetry. Like fiction, poetry tells us stories, but they are stories in miniature. The poet leaves it to you to open the work and see his or her world in which you, too, live.

THE ELEMENTS OF POETRY

When you have come to feel the importance of a poet and the special qualities of his or her work, you have reached the stage where you should be capable of writing critical essays about that work. However, critical writing requires that you deal with the major elements of poetry, which are detailed in the following section.

Types of Poetry

Broadly and structurally speaking there are two basic kinds of poetry. The first and by far the more traditional, is the "closed" form, which follows a pattern that we may find in a sonnet or villanelle, "heroic" or "blank" verse *(verso sciolto)*. Closed poetry abides by rules of form set down long ago and rarely departs from them. These rules determine the length of each line, and where rhyme and accent are placed. Of course, as poetry evolved, various authors experimented with the traditional forms.

The "open" form, often called "free verse" or *vers libre,* is considered to be an American-created form as opposed to the closed forms, which are European. The open form relies heavily not on rhyme and not necessarily on the traditional metric feet that create rhythm, but on a perhaps more subtle rhythm called "cadence," and imagery.

Beneath the headings of closed and open are many types of poetry, easily a dozen or even more, which are variations of three major styles in poetry: narrative (treated earlier in this chapter), dramatic monologue, and lyric. Matthew Arnold characterized the monologue as being "The dialogue of the mind with itself." Believed to be popular only since the Middle Ages, it nevertheless is rooted much deeper in the poetic imagination, back to the epics and sagas and papyri, to the Greek plays, which are written in poetry. Everyone knows the beginning of Hamlet's soliloquy (or monologue)—"To be or not to be," spoken while Hamlet ponders revenge. The critical situations of characters in all literature have always been the ideal times for them to range about within themselves for solutions. In the following example of dramatic monologue, Alfred, Lord Tennyson places "Ulysses" in a very special place located between the allegorical renderings of Dante and the myths related by the Homerian *Iliad* and *Odyssey.* In this section, Ulysses from afar contemplates the virtues and perhaps defects in his son:

> This is my son, mine own Telemachus,
> To whom I leave the sceptre and the isle—
> Well-loved of me, discerning to fulfil
> This labour, by slow prudence to make mild
> A rugged people, and thro' soft degrees
> Subdue them to the useful and the good.
> Most blameless is he, centered in the sphere

> Of common duties, decent not to fail
> In offices of tenderness, and pay
> Meet adoration to my household gods,
> When I am gone. He works his work, I mine.

"Ulysses" is in blank verse—metered in iambic pentameter without rhyme. It is a closed poem.

Lyric poetry is distinguished by the personal posture of the poet—how he or she views the world. The language is strong yet plain and striking. We are made aware of the world around us through the personification of the elements of which it is composed. Yet lyric poetry is controlled through its structure which defines it, too, as closed, as we see in Wordsworth's "Composed Upon Westminster Bridge, September 3, 1802":

> Earth has not anything to show more fair:
> Dull would be he of soul who could pass by
> A sight so touching in its majesty:
> This city now doth, like a garment, wear
> The beauty of the morning; silent, bare,
> Ships, towers, domes, theatres, and temples lie
> Open unto the fields, and to the sky;
> All bright and glittering in the smokeless air.
> Never did the sun more beautifully steep
> In his first splendour, valley, rock, or hill;
> Ne'er saw I, never felt, a calm so deep!
> The river glideth at his own sweet will:
> Dear God! the very houses seem asleep;
> And all that mighty heart is lying still!

William Wordsworth became the standard-bearer of lyric poetry (lyric: "fit to be sung with a lyre or harp"), with his 1798 publication of *Lyrical Ballads* (first edition; there were three). By contrast, in the United States Walt Whitman "said his 'God be with you' to the European poets and then parted company with them irrevocably . . . and with his American colleagues, too. He sang no sweet songs, but long, loosely metered chants," wrote critic Max Herzberg. *Leaves of Grass* was Whitman's mark upon the land and mind of America in 1855, and, shortly after, the world.

An example of Whitman's innovative open poetry is his "Cavalry Crossing a Ford," set during the Civil War:

> A line in long array where they wind betwixt green islands,
> They take a serpentine course, their arms flash in the sun—hark to the musical
>   clank,
> Behold the silvery river, in it the splashing horses loitering stop to drink,
> Behold the brown-faced men, each group, each person a picture, the negligent rest
>   on the saddles,
> Some emerge on the opposite bank, others are just entering the ford—while,
> Scarlet and blue and snowy white,
> The guidon flags flutter gayly in the wind.

"Calvary Crossing a Ford" contains very long lines and some short lines. Basically, the language is not used to yield thundering interior or metric rhythms. Like a serpent ("serpentine course"), the cavalry winds from one bank of the river to the other. The emphasis is on alliteration, the repetition of consonant or vowel sounds at the beginning of words: "A line in long array"; "emerge . . . opposite . . . others . . . entering . . . flags flutter . . . ."; "Scarlet and blue and snowy white" not only is alliterative, but has a subtle rhythm as well. The intent of this open poem is to create a picture through word images, and a single picture usually captures one event in progress, "narrates" one story that opens on a wider world. In this case that world is the Civil War.

Voice and Tone

Tone is the "voice" or attitude we encounter in a poem. Tone tells us the way the poet feels about you, himself or herself, the world. Gwendolyn Brooks' diction in "The Bean Eaters" is designed to make us feel a very particular way:

> They eat beans mostly, this old yellow pair.
> Dinner is a casual affair.
> Plain chipware on a plain and creaking wood,
> Tin flatware.
>
> Two who are Mostly Good.
> Two have lived their day,
> But keep on putting on their clothes
> And putting things away.
>
> And remembering . . .
> Remembering, with twinklings and twinges,
> As they lean over the beans in their rented back room that
>   is full of beads and receipts and dolls and cloths,
> Tobacco crumbs, vases and fringes.

Describe the tone of "The Bean Eaters." Note the several images that highlight the condition of these elderly people, and the empathy Brooks expresses. In some ways there is a similarity between the determination of the couple to "keep on" doing things and Ulysses' pledge "to strive, to seek, to find and not to yield" (in the final stanza). In Brooks' poem, also note the structure with both short and long lines, and rhyme, though it is irregular. Is the poem open, closed, or a combination of both?

Note the differences in tone—attitude—and structure between Brooks' poem and Cyn. Zarco's poem:

> Asparagus
>
> There's a washcloth
> with a picture of asparagus
> in my bathroom.

Did you know
that Filipinos were picked
to grow asparagus in the West
because they were short
and built close to the ground?

I'm 5'3". I don't use
that washcloth anymore.

There is a cleanness and brevity of line in this poem that contains a tone of de-
fiance about the past—and the future. It is an open, lyrical poem, but you have
to fill in some of the story.

Sound is frequently associated with voice and tone. But the creation of
sound in a poem, that is, making you seem to hear sound, is a process of diction. Poets select certain words that we have come to associate with certain
sounds. "Splash," "buzz," and "hiss," for example, are commonly associated
with water, flying insects, geese, and serpents. The Greek word *onomatopoeia*
simply means naming a thing or action by imitating it vocally. Sound often
may be sensed in the way a poem is written, for example in Coleridge's
"Kubla Khan," before we are actually aware of the sound. But do remember
that most poets think about sound because their work traditionally was heard,
not read, although there is much poetry written today primarily to be read.
The utilization of rhythm, meter, alliteration, assonance, and dissonance (see
the glossary in your anthology) are crucial in producing sound in a poem.

Imagery and Symbolism

Poetry would not be poetry without imagery (words and phrases that address
the senses) and symbolism (words that evoke additional meanings beyond
their literal significance). Homer gives us the "rosy-fingered dawn" and the
"wine-dark sea," images that have lingered more than 2,000 years. An image,
may be created with one or several related words used to make us feel that we
are "living in a poem" through hearing, feeling, tasting, seeing, or smelling.

The Symbolist movement began in France late in the nineteenth century.
Its members believed poetry could better express and explore the human psyche by recreating human consciousness through symbols, which often reflect
inexpressible emotions. In the United States, the "Imagists" were the American counterparts of the Symbolists.

Sometimes the major image in a poem is indicated by its title, as in Imagist
Amy Lowell's "Taxi":

When I go away from you
The world beats dead
Like a slackened drum.
I call out for you against the jutted stars
And shout into the ridges of the wind.
Streets coming fast,
One after the other,

Wedge you away from me.
And the lamps of the city prick my eyes
So that I can no longer see your face.
Why should I leave you,
To wound myself upon the sharp edges of the night?

All the related images employed here define a situation. What is it, what's going on? How does the text of the poem fracture the "I" and "you" found in five of the twelve lines? Is this an open or closed poem?

In poetry (and fiction) the function of symbolism is to stand for a state of mind instead of representing a specific object. For example, in everyday life, we know that the green light tells us that we may walk across the street, while the red one advises us not to. The red, white, and blue flag with thirteen stripes and fifty stars is a symbol having many meanings to Americans. If the flag were green with black stripes and red stars it would have very little meaning for most of us because, as Kenneth Burke wrote, "A symbol is the verbal parallel to a pattern of experience," and our experiences have prepared us not for green, black, and red, but red, white, and blue, the flag that stands for the United States of America.

Some poets take standard symbols and create new ones that have reference to the old, familiar ones. For it is in the nature of poetry to create newer and possibly more accurate symbols for the world we know. The first and final stanzas of Gerald Vizenor's "Haiku" offer us familiar symbols with uncommon meanings:

october sunflowers
like rows of defeated soldiers
leaning in the frost

october wind
garage doors open and close
wings of the moth

Although the term "image" calls up something we have seen, in poetic terms we are considering specific, related words that have to do with sensual (the five senses) experiences.

A symbol, on the other hand, stands for something other than what it is.

Simile and Metaphor

A simile is a figure of speech that compares two things from different categories, using signal words such as "like," "as," and "seems." A metaphor also makes a comparison between unlike things but without these signal words.

"Johnson is as tall as Bird" is *not* a simile, but "Johnson is as tall as a small tree" is, because of the dissimilarity of the references or comparisons. Similes use "like" or "as"—"He ran like the wind." Metaphors also substitute one thing for another, hence "tree" for "Bird." Aristotle believed that the ability to find resemblance in disparate things was "the best gift of the poet."

In Maya Angelou's "To a Husband" we find powerful metaphors in the opening lines:

> Your voice at times a fist
> > Tight in your throat
> Jabs ceaselessly at phantoms
> > In the room,
> Your hand a carved and
> > Skimming boat
> Goes down the Nile
> > To point out Pharaoh's tomb.

Note the absence of "like" in the first and fifth lines of the stanza.

Analogy is often associated with simile and metaphor. It presumes a resemblance between two things. This example is from Francis Bacon: "*Money* is like *muck,* not good unless it's spread." *Allusion,* also to be found in this company, is an indirect reference to some person, place, object, or event within a literary work. Babette Deutsch's poem, "Disasters of War: Goya at the Museum," alludes to a famous painting by Francisco y Lucientes Goya (1746–1828) that hangs in the Prado Museum in Madrid.

Diction and Syntax

Diction is the conscious manipulation of language. It has been described as the clothes words wear. But, since words wear out with use and become cliché, for permanence as well as poetic sensibility, diction should suggest rather than state. And the use of symbolism, metaphor, and simile, which in themselves require linguistic knowledge and dexterity, can only be effective through judicious diction—the selection and use of poetic language.

Syntax is the way words are organized in order to have meaning; words so formed become sentences and phrases, which in turn can become poems, stories, novels, or plays, or today's big newspaper story. The word selection or diction in Octavio Paz's "Engaged" is supported by a syntax that seems deceptively repetitious:

> Stretching out on the grass
> a boy and a girl.
> Sucking their oranges, giving kisses
> like waves exchanging foam.
>
> Stretched out on the beach
> a boy and a girl.
> Sucking their limes, giving their kisses
> like clouds exchanging foam.
>
> Stretched out underground
> a boy and a girl.
> Saying nothing, never kissing,
> giving silence for silence.

The poet has described, with slight differences, places where there are always "stretched out" "a boy and a girl," who are "giving" their kisses until the final stanza. Then the first and last two lines surprise. We want to say at the end, "Wait a minute," and reread the poem to absorb that final difference, not so much in the syntax, which led us there, as much as the *place* that makes the disruption in behavior, tone, and meaning. Note the similes within the syntax.

Meter and Rhythm

In Greek, meter means *metron* or measure. Most consistently used in closed poetry (which need not necessarily be "traditional"), meter is the regular recurrence of a pattern of rhythm or rhythms in lines of poetry; meter is the beat we can relate to just as in music. If you think of the poems you remember best, you might discover that they were rhythmical as well as rhymed. Critic John Middleton Murry wrote: "There is a background of metrical sameness separating us like a curtain from the practical world; there is a richness of rhythmical variation to make the world in which we are, worthy of attention." Rhythm is formed by the stress (or accent or beat) on certain syllables within what are called "feet" in lines of poetry. Some words are naturally stressed, others naturally not, so another function of diction is not only to select the right words to make the point of the poem, but to select the right ones with the right stress or lack thereof. In poetry written in English, the typical metrical feet are *iambic* ($\breve{}\,'$), *trochaic* ($'\breve{}$), *anapestic* ($\breve{}\breve{}\,'$), and *dactylic* ($'\breve{}\breve{}$). *Scansion* is the method of analyzing the kind of meter and number of feet used in a poetic line.

Ben Jonson's "Still to Be Neat," which follows, is an example of a rhythmical (and rhymed) poem containing precisely four feet in each line but with interesting metrical variation. Try "scanning" each line.

> Still to be neat, still to be drest,
> As you were going to a feast;
> Still to be pou'dred, still perfum'd:
> Lady, it is to be presum'd,
> Though arts hid causes are not found
> All is not sweet, all is not sound.
>
> Give me a look, give me a face,
> That makes simplicity a grace;
> Robes loosely flowing, hair as free:
> Such sweet neglect more taketh me,
> Than all th'adulteries of art.
> They strike mine eyes, but not mine heart.

You wonder if Jonson is writing about Art or Woman—or both—here, but it is the striking control of meter that creates the rhythm that in the first place entraps us in the poem long enough to examine its theme.

Theme

As indicated in the section on fiction, theme is the essence of subject, which is more general. In that section, poet Wilfred Owen was contrasted with fiction writers Tolstoy and Hemingway. Here is another poet, perhaps the greatest,

William Shakespeare, who within the constraints of the fourteen-line sonnet (number 116), addresses the durability of true love:

> Let me not to the marriage of true minds
> Admit impediments. Love is not love
> Which alters when it alteration finds,
> Or bends with the remover to remove:
> O, no; it is an ever-fixèd mark,
> That looks on tempests and is never shaken:
> It is the star to every wandering bark,
> Whose worth's unknown, although his height be taken.
> Love's not Time's fool, though rosy lips and cheeks
> Within his bending sickle's compass come;
> Love alters not with his brief hours and weeks,
> But bears it out even to the edge of doom.
>   If this be error and upon me proved,
>   I never writ, nor no man ever loved.

Themes in literature provide us with the tools we require for understanding a work. But theme is never stated; we arrive at it through action and insight when we have worked our way inside a story, novel, or poem.

INTERPRETING POETRY

When we say "work our way inside," we mean *knowing* a work of literature as well as we can. Reading and rereading a poem, aloud as well as silently, is one step to interpreting poetry. Another, as in fiction, is to know under what circumstances a poem was written. This, of course, additionally means knowing something about the author, and the more the better since, obviously, poems do not write themselves. Exercising your knowledge of the elements of poetry is a crucial factor in interpretation.

While there can be several interpretations of a work, there are always common elements that writers consider. Decide what kind of poetry is under discussion, dramatic monologue, lyric, or narrative (or a combination of them). Are you writing about closed poetry with its traditional rules, or open poetry which tends to make its own rules? Unlike a story, remember, a poem will render a great theme down to its essences, its most important aspects. Critical analysis requires that, early on in your paper, you state clearly what the theme is. Once you know that, you can then find the elements in the poem to support your opinion that the theme is what you think it is. If you are right, discuss the clues that led you to this conclusion, the words, the images, the lines and their formations.

Should your assignment be to compare two poems, the process is essentially the same. For example, given Shelley's "Ozymandias" and Coleridge's "Kubla Khan," you might arrive at somewhat similar themes that suggest, in sinister fashion, a warning to humankind. Both are set in unworldly locations; both possess an ominous, sometimes eerie tone, yet both are by lyrical poets who use meter, rhythm, and rhyme to convey meaning. The most obvious point of *contrast*, on the other hand, is in the length of the two poems, the brevity of Shelley's, and the length and growth of power in Coleridge's.

Although Coleridge was born twenty years before Shelley, who drowned at 30, both were influenced by Wordsworthian ideals and the philosophies of the Age of Reason, which are other comparisons you can make. Coleridge died at 62, but the lines in his "Kubla Khan" remain, as Rudyard Kipling said, "the most magical in the English language."

EVALUATING POETRY

If your instinct for liking what is good has served you well, trust it now. That is the starting place for evaluating a poem. A good poem should have meaning for you; it should make you think or wonder—and then think and wonder again about its content.

Not all poetry, however, is good, even if it has been published, but it still may be worthy of your consideration. If you examine rhythm or cadence in a closed or open poem, you should be critical of the poet's ability to maintain the beat; if it has broken down without any plausible reason, perhaps the poet tired of maintaining it, or forgot to. This failure might be one that caused you not to like the poem, though you may not have known the reason why.

If a poem has relied heavily on images you do not understand, or offers no hope whatsoever of being made clear, your evaluation will of course be negative, and rightly so. (Some poets work hard not to be understood.) Other poets, while seemingly accessible, are more subtle with the elements they employ, and you may find their work seductive. A poem with an abundance of metaphors or similes is one with too many images. On the other hand, a poem stingy with these and other elements that poetry requires may offer too little to engage you. Imprecise diction may echo like a wrong note played on a musical instrument, but recall that it was the precision of most of the diction that called your attention to the imprecision in the first place. Look for what bounces best off your own sensibilities, taking note of the advice suggested above. It may be worth knowing that for many poets, a poem remains an unfinished work; he or she will often go back to even an already published work in some cases and change something in it, which he or she believes will make it better. For most of us, good poetry makes us feel a way we cannot always explain other than to say, "good."

CHAPTER 5

Writing about Drama

"All the world's a stage," wrote Shakespeare, and on that stage we witness the joys and sorrows, the tragedy and comedy, the reality and romance of life. While one traditional purpose of drama is to "suspend your sense of disbelief" so that you can respond emotionally to what you experience, thinking about and describing drama gives you a far deeper understanding of it. Learning about tragedy, comedy, tragicomedy, melodrama, and other types of plays will help you understand the conventions of dramatic literature and playwriting, and through this process, help you to not only experience the world of the play, but aid you in understanding *why* you experience it the way you do.

THE ELEMENTS OF DRAMA

Tragedy and comedy are the best-known categories of dramatic writing perhaps because they were the first to be defined, and have a long, if somewhat erratic, tradition. Aristotle, in his *Poetics*, describes and defines the nature of tragedy, albeit his view was limited because he based it upon tragedy written during the "golden age" of Greek drama, and obviously could not foretell the evolution of the drama through the millennia to follow. But the prolific writings of Aeschylus, Sophocles, and Euripides—the three Greek tragedians whose plays remain extant—provided Aristotle with enough samples to devise a theory of tragic form. For Aristotle, tragedy focused on a hero (male or female) of noble birth, who, through a misdeed or *hamartia*, underwent a decline in stature that led to tragic consequences whether in the realm of material prosperity, physical well-being, or moral rectitude, or a combination of these, as in the case of *Oedipus Rex*. Even the titles of many Greek tragedies are the royal personages upon which the plays focus, such as *Antigone, Electra,* and *Agamemnon.*

The development and subsequent action of true tragedy usually derives from one or more of three possible modes of conflict: an internal conflict that the protagonist, or main character, must resolve within himself or herself; a conflict between a protagonist and an outside antagonist; or one between the protagonist and the society-at-large. Although the play *A Raisin in the Sun* by Lorraine Hansberry might not be classified as a classic tragedy, it embodies all those conflicts that make tragedy possible. Walter Younger is confronted by several simultaneous conflicts. He is at odds with his family who have different ideas concerning how to spend his father's life insurance benefits. He is in conflict with society-at-large in the guise of Mr. Linder, who offers to buy back the home in a white neighborhood that the Younger family has just purchased, rather than allow the African-American family to move in. Finally, he must do battle with his own sense of righteousness and justice, whether to accept the offer that will leave him with enough money to open his liquor store, and tacitly accept the racist motivation behind it; or keep the newly purchased house, and struggle to make a decent life for his family. Most drama that has been acknowledged through history as the finest examples of the playwright's art (such plays as *A Doll's House, Oedipus,* and *Death of a Salesman,* as well as most of the works of Shakespeare) interweave these three elements of conflict.

On the stage today, we rarely see a contemporary tragedy that rigidly conforms to the genre as it was first defined by Aristotle. First of all, few of us truly would be shocked by flaws in so-called great personages, as we have come to consider even the loftiest world leaders as human and subject to the same weaknesses as the rest of us. Tabloids are filled with sordid tales of great men and women and we have grown to take them for granted. Second, playwrights, beginning in the nineteenth century, have broadened their perspective to focus attention on the conflicts and actions of the lower and middle classes, not just the mighty and powerful. One might call this the democratization of tragedy, and this inclination has followed the same trends that have occurred in other art forms, for example, painting, poetry, architecture, and so on. Take for example the very name of the main protagonist in Arthur Miller's *Death of a Salesman*—where "Low-man" suggests his humble status.

Coinciding with the reduction in the stature of characters in tragedy has come a hybrid form that has come to be known as tragicomedy, that is, works of drama that combine the tragic and comic together. *A Raisin in the Sun* combines elements of both tragic and comic form as do David Hwang's *Family Devotions* and Susan Glaspell's *Suppressed Desires*. While these plays address issues such as intergenerational and intercultural conflict, rancor, jealousy, even murder, the playwrights have managed to inject moments of humor that add dimension to human experience.

We do not have a comprehensive theory of comedy from Aristotle (although he planned to write one), but we do have many early extant Greek comedies by the playwright Aristophanes who poked fun at Greek mores, politics, and society. Perhaps his most famous play is *Lysistrata,* which satirizes the absurdity of war as well as the "war between the sexes." Today, political satire is alive and well in film and television, and as you probably know, is a major subject for contemporary stand-up comedians.

The two Roman comic writers whose works are extant are Terence and Plautus. They helped to initiate the type of theater we know as comedy. Influenced by the Greeks, Plautus' plays satirized Roman life, using such devices as bungling behavior, reversals of expectations, and mistaken identity to keep his audience laughing. His most famous play, *The Menaechmi Twins*, was the inspiration for Shakespeare's first play, *The Comedy of Errors*. And today we still see the influence of Roman comedy in such forms as farce and slapstick in the theater and situation comedies on TV. Terence's comedies, on the other hand, did not go for the broad laugh, and just as is true among today's audiences, his more subtle comedies and humanistic themes were not as popular as Plautus', whose work inspired more belly laughs.

Melodrama is a type of drama which, although derived from tragedy, stands apart from it because the conflicts that the characters must confront are contrived or merely clever and the characters are usually less fleshed out than three-dimensional dramatic characters, and they seem to resolve their conflicts in interesting, yet concocted ways. While melodrama is not found as much on the stage today as it was in the nineteenth century, the form is alive and well in many contemporary action-adventure movies like the *Indiana Jones* films and *Romancing the Stone*, where men and women are saved from disaster in the nick of time, much as they are in the old cliché of the damsel in distress who is tied to a railroad track as a speeding train approaches, only to be whisked away at the last moment by a valiant hero.

With the proliferation of drama portraying the common person, many audience members have become accustomed to associating plays with realistic portraits of life and with rather conventional ways of depicting such portraits, as though the theater were a place to see a mirror or reproduction of real life. This couldn't be further from the truth, however. Many so-called schools and movements of drama have depicted life in unrealistic manners. Playwrights such as Eugene Ionesco and Samuel Beckett portray a world that is quite unlike the one with which we are familiar. Plays representing life with an unreal quality include depictions of life as romantic as in Lady Gregory's *The Rising of the Moon;* or absurd as in Samuel Beckett's *Krapp's Last Tape;* or magical as in Langston Hughes' *Soul Gone Home*. Even the contemporary classic *Death of a Salesman* has many scenes of unreality, when, for example, Willie's brother seems to magically appear on stage much in the same way as the ghost appears in *Hamlet*.

Plot

As in fiction, plot is essential to nearly all drama, in fact, possibly more so than to other forms of literature. Plot is a skeleton of the action in a play. It is what happens to characters under the circumstances the playwright has devised. One reason plot is so important in drama is that since plays are meant to be performed and seen, an audience will have little tolerance for pauses in the action. In fiction, on the other hand, action may be interwoven with physical description or characters' thoughts. In drama, what you see is what you get, so to speak. And it is the playwright, in his or her division of acts and scenes, who will determine the pauses in the action, whereas a reader is free to stop and start reading where he or she pleases.

To keep the plot of a drama interesting to its audience, most playwrights try to maintain a heightened level of action through the development of conflicts and obstacles that occur far more readily and densely than they do in real life. It is through such conflict that the plot moves forward. And the greater the stakes involved in these conflicts, the more riveting the play will be and the more you will care about how the conflict is resolved. Take for example an early scene in *A Doll's House* by Henrik Ibsen. Nora, the protagonist, is having a discussion with Krogstad, a man from whom she borrowed money to keep her family intact during a stressful and tenuous period. Krogstad, a bank clerk, fearing that he will be passed by for a promotion by his superior, Helmer (Nora's husband), threatens to blackmail Nora by revealing that she borrowed money from him without her husband's knowledge.

KROGSTAD: . . . My sons are growing up; for their sake, I must try to regain what respectability I can. This job in the bank was the first step on the ladder. And now your husband wants to kick me off that ladder into the dirt.

NORA: But my dear Mr. Krogstad, it simply isn't in my power to help you.

KROGSTAD: You say that because you don't want to help me. But I have the means to make you.

NORA: You don't mean you'd tell my husband that I owe you money?

KROGSTAD: And if I did?

NORA: That' be a filthy trick!

Nora counters that her husband will merely pay back the money that is owed, which would at first glance seem to defuse Krogstad's threat. But Krogstad retaliates and increases the stakes and the conflict by dangling a damaging secret about Nora's loan before her. Several lines later, the following exchange occurs:

KROGSTAD: I promised to get you the money in exchange for an I.O.U., which I drew up.

NORA: Yes, and which I signed.

KROGSTAD: Exactly. But then I added a few lines naming your father as security for the debt. This paragraph was to be signed by your father.

NORA: Was to be? He did sign it.

• • •

KROGSTAD: Tell me, Mrs. Helmer, do you by any chance remember the date of your father's death? The day of the month, I mean.

NORA: Papa died on the twenty-ninth of September.

KROGSTAD: Quite correct; I took the trouble to confirm it. And that leaves me with a curious little problem—[*Takes a paper.*] which I simply cannot solve.

NORA: Problem? I don't see—

KROGSTAD: The problem, Mrs. Helmer, is that your father signed this paper three days after his death.

This building and relaxing and building again of tension is what moves the action of the play forward, giving shape to the plot.

   While the building up of tension in this example is fairly clear, what seems
to be mere conversation in a play often contains the seeds of conflict that will
have an impact on the later action. This is particularly true of more contemporary plays that portray human action in subtler terms. Take for example one of
the many conflicts that beset the Younger family in *A Raisin in the Sun*—the
conflict between Walter's ambitions and the caution of his wife, Ruth. It is evident even in this bit of morning banter from Act I:

WALTER: You know what I was thinking 'bout in the bathroom this morning?
RUTH: No!
WALTER: How come you always try to be so pleasant?
RUTH: What is there to be pleasant 'bout?
WALTER: You want to know what I was thinking 'bout in the bathroom or
          not?
RUTH: I know what you thinking 'bout.
WALTER: 'Bout what me and Willy Harris was talking about last night.
RUTH: Willy Harris is a good-for-nothing loudmouth.

We eventually learn that Willy Harris is involving Walter in a scheme to open
up a liquor store, and this has a dramatic impact on Walter's actions during
the play, initiating a complex series of conflicts between himself and other
members of his family.

   While plays rely on rising action that is a result of tensions that in turn are
caused by a conflict or a series of conflicts, this conflict must somehow be resolved or at least relieved in the end. It is unlikely that you would feel satisfied with a plot that left a major conflict unresolved. As in most plays, the climax to the rising action in *A Raisin in the Sun* occurs near its end. In this
poignant scene, Walter's internal and external conflicts are resolved in a showdown with Mr. Linder when the latter pays his final visit to purchase back a
house the Younger family has bought in a white neighborhood:

WALTER: Yeah, Well—what I mean is that we come from people who had a
          lot of *pride*. I mean—we are very proud people. And that's my sister
          over there and she's going to be a doctor—and we are very proud—
LINDER: Well—I am sure that is very nice, but—
WALTER: What I am telling you is that we called you over here to tell you that
          we are very proud and that this—Travis, come here. This is my son,
          and he makes the sixth generation our family in this country. And
          we have all thought about your offer—
LINDER: Well, good . . . good—
WALTER: And we have decided to move into our house because my father—
          my father—he earned it for us brick by brick. We don't want to
          make no trouble for nobody or fight no causes, and we will try to be
          good neighbors. And that's *all* we got to say about that. We don't
          want your money.

The Younger family's conflict now resolved, the play ends with them banter-
ing happily about their move, their spirits uplifted. As you read a play, keep
in mind the importance of plot and make notes on how the plot develops. To

learn more about plot, you may also want to predict how the plot unfolds, and compare your idea with that of the author's.

Character

Aristotle suggested and playwrights in general follow the rule of thumb that "character is action." Another way of thinking about character is to envision him or her as determined by the choices he or she makes. Take the character of Iago from *Othello*. In the character list he is described as "IAGO, Othello's ensign, a villain." This does not tell us very much. However, in the first Scene of *Othello*, we soon find out what kind of person he is. Othello, it appears, has passed over Iago for promotion to lieutenant. Iago is enraged, for—as far as he is concerned—he has the greater experience in matters of war than the candidate Othello has demonstrated. He states his feelings to Roderigo this way:

> Preferment goes by letter and affection,
> And not by old graduation, where each second
> Stood heir to th' first. Now, sir, be judge yourself,
> Whether I in any just term am affined
> To love the Moor.

During the course of the play, Iago's character is revealed as he methodically torments Othello until the latter thinks Desdemona, his wife, has been unfaithful, resulting in the demise of both Othello and his wife. While most of us would like to take revenge upon a seemingly unfair boss, few of us would act upon it as Iago does. Understanding the traits that make character interesting is what allowed Shakespeare to appeal to an audience that was made up of all social classes. So, despite the fact that Shakespeare is renowned for the quality of his language, it is his talent for developing character that makes him a good playwright.

This focus on the relationship between action and character should not give you the impression that a three-dimensional character is fully developed through his or her actions alone or that it is easy to develop a dramatic character. For a character to behave plausibly throughout a play, the playwright must have a strong sense of who that character is, how the character looks, sounds, dresses, thinks, reacts, and so on. Henrik Ibsen, one of the fathers of modern drama (perhaps because of his ability to create such well-motivated characters) said this about the people who inhabited his plays:

> Before I write down one word, I have to have the character in mind through and through, and I must penetrate into the last part of his soul—the individual comes before anything else—the stage set, etc. . . .

The most interesting characters in drama tend to be complex ones, and their actions although seemingly truthful may not necessarily be anticipated ones. Who would think that the Sergeant in Lady Gregory's *The Rising of the Moon* would let the fugitive go or that Othello would kill his wife or that Willy Loman, despite his pathetic nature, would kill himself so his family could be sustained by his insurance money, or that Oedipus would blind himself? All these actions are credible, but unexpected. In writing about character, ask yourself questions. Most likely they are the same sorts of questions the playwright asked as he or she planned to write. Who is this character? What are the given circumstances of time, place, social class, and situation that he or she must respond to? How does he or she respond?

Not all characters in plays are so fully developed that you will feel you know all about them. Many plays are populated by characters who enter the stage for a small portion of the play. These are often called "secondary characters." But a talented playwright will have even secondary characters. For example, Sylvester, Ma Rainey's nephew in August Wilson's *Ma Rainey's Black Bottom,* is fleshed out, interesting, and a contributing factor in the action of the play, having been endowed with a puerile personality and a noticeable stutter.

Setting

Unlike the movies, where you may be transported from New York to California to Tokyo in the blink of an eye, the settings in plays remain rather static throughout the action, changing perhaps between acts, if at all. And also unlike movies, which can actually show us all the minutiae of life by directly filming it, settings in drama often only suggest the places they depict, or, if it is in the playwright's vision, even distort them. Still other playwrights may not consider setting important at all, and their plays are often devoid of any description as to how the stage should be depicted, leaving it up to you, the reader or playgoer, to fill in the gaps with your imagination.

Besides revealing time and place through props (furniture, everyday objects, and costuming), setting can also exploit stage lighting and special effects such as rear-projected film and sound effects to enhance the mood of a play. Dim lighting might suggest a depressing atmosphere; bright lights, an upbeat one. Advances in theatrical technology have expanded the possibilities of establishing setting, as they have our expectations of how setting is depicted. The Greeks relied upon the simplest of means to suggest time and place—for example, a vertical rectangular box that was painted with a tree on one side, an architectural column on the other (which would be turned according to whether the scene was set in the city or the countryside). Contemporary playwrights, on the other hand, have often called for fairly elaborate staging so that the audience actually sees a fair representation of the place it is meant to depict. In the end, however, the complexity or lack thereof of a setting is usually up to the vision of the playwright. Notice, for example, the opening setting from the contemporary playwright David Hwang's *Family Devotions.*

> The sunroom and backyard of a home in Bel Air. Everywhere is glass—glass roof, glass walls. Upstage of the lanai/sunroom is a patio with a barbecue and a tennis court. The tennis court leads offstage. As the curtain rises, we see a single spotlight on an old Chinese face and hear Chinese music or chanting. Suddenly, the music becomes modern-day funk or rock 'n' roll, and the lights

come up to reveal the set. The face is that of DI-GOU, an older Chinese man wearing a blue suit and carrying an old suitcase. He is peering into the sunroom from the tennis court, through the glass walls. Behind him, a stream of black smoke is coming from the barbecue.

Another function of setting that may perform an important role in the life of a play is its ability to suggest the mood of the environment and/or reveal aspects of the character's or characters' interior emotions. Note Lorraine Hansberry's use of personification in her description of the Younger household at the start of *A Raisin in the Sun,* a description that provides you with an insight into the emotional tenor of the occupants.

> Its furnishings are typical and undistinguished and their primary feature now is that they have clearly had to accommodate the living of too many people for too many years—and they are tired. . . . Now the once loved pattern of the couch upholstery has *to fight to show itself* from under acres of crocheted doilies and couch covers . . . but the *carpet has fought back by showing its weariness,* with depressing uniformity, elsewhere on its surface.

Thus, the setting mirrors the Younger family's life circumstances and their interior lives as well, and at the same time provides an introduction to the play that may rivet your attention and make you want to read more.

The description of setting that introduces Arthur Miller's *Death of a Salesman* produces a similar effect in providing an analogy between Willy's home and its environs and Willy's state of mind in relationship to *his* environment. It is interesting to note that Miller's original title for the play was "The Inside of His Head."

> We are aware of towering, angular shapes behind it, surrounding it on all sides. Only the blue light of the sky falls upon the house and forestage; the surrounding area shows an angry glow of orange. As more light appears, we see a solid vault of apartment houses around the small, fragile-seeming home. An air of the dream clings to the place, a dream rising out of reality.

Staging

Plays are meant to be performed and for audiences to view the performances. If you've ever read a play and then gone to see it performed, you probably became aware of the difference between the two experiences. Seeing a performance of a play is what makes it complete. While you can ascertain certain things from reading plays that you would be hard pressed to do from a performance, for example, arcane references in the dialogue, subtleties of style, camouflaged symbols and the like, being present at a performance of a play adds a dimension to your understanding and appreciation of drama that is impossible from reading.

In staging a play, the theater artist has to consider such elements as casting, makeup, costume, the arrangement and movement of the actors on the stage (referred to as blocking), physical and vocal pacing, vocal qualities—in fact, nearly anything that contributes to communicating the world of the play to the mind of the audience member. While nothing can substitute for seeing a live performance, one way to envision what a play would be like performed when you read it is to imagine how you would see it at a performance. For example, how do you imagine Nora to look in *A Doll's House*? How does Othello or Oedipus carry himself? Is the former tall, short; does he possess a serious demeanor? How is the latter dressed? Oedipus is supposed to have a misshapen foot. How do you imagine him to walk? What sorts of facial and body expressions do the musicians carry in *Ma Rainey's Black Bottom*? Do they appear angry, resigned, frustrated, etc.? It is important for you to consider that while a play in manuscript form is made up of words on a page, the stage is a physical and visual space that must be filled and kept interesting through props, costume, movement, activity, vocal character, lighting, and sound.

Dialogue

When you read a play, particularly a contemporary one like *A Raisin in the Sun* or *Ma Rainey's Black Bottom,* chances are you find the dialogue similar to everyday speech, which is casual, colloquial, and conversational. If so, the playwright is doing a good job at giving you the *illusion* that dialogue is like the daily conversations each of us has. Actually, good dialogue is distilled speech and is structured so that it consistently contributes to the creation or resolution of conflict, moving the action of the play forward, or enlightening us about character. What might appear to you as mere transposition of speech from a tape recorder to the page is actually a craft that requires a keen sense of language and its rhythms. A playwright may very well write and rewrite a play many times until he or she gets it right. One playwright, in a humorous mood, once offered a $10,000 reward for anyone who could show him a tape recorder that recorded dramatic dialogue from real life.

Read the following dialogue from *The Rising of the Moon* by Lady Gregory, and consider how it contributes to the drama:

POLICEMAN B: I think this would be a good place to put up a notice. [*He points to barrel.*]
POLICEMAN X: Better ask him. [*Calls to* SERGEANT.] Will this be a good place for a placard?

[*No answer.*]

POLICEMAN B: Will we put up a notice here on the barrel?

[*No answer.*]

SERGEANT: There's a flight of steps here that leads to the water. This is a place that should be minded well. If he got down there, his friends might have a boat to meet him; they might send it in here from outside.
POLICEMAN B: Would the barrel be a good place to put a notice up?
SERGEANT: It might; you can put it there.

[*They pass the notice up.*]

SERGEANT:	[*Reading it.*] Dark hair—dark eyes, smooth face, height five feet five—there's not much to take hold of in that—It's a pity I had no chance of seeing him before he broke out of gaol. They say he's a wonder, that it's he makes all the plans for the whole organization. There isn't another man in Ireland would have broken gaol the way he did. He must have some friends among the gaolers.
POLICEMAN B:	A hundred pounds is little enough for the Government to offer for him. You may be sure any man in the force that takes him will get promotion.
SERGEANT:	I'll mind this place myself. I wouldn't wonder at all if he came this way.

In only a few sentences, this dialogue establishes a number of important dramatic issues. It establishes the locale. It provides us an understanding of the characters' motivations for their actions. It sets up the mood since the police reveal through their observations that they are in a strange part of the city, making their actions tentative. Their subordinate relationship to the sergeant, their supervisor, is established. Note too that there are pauses in the dialogue when the two police call and the sergeant does not respond. What do you think is implied by the fact that the sergeant does not respond? What do you think is implied by the fact that the sergeant does not answer them? How do the pauses contribute to the mood? Anton Chekhov, the great Russian playwright, used pauses in the dialogue to great psychological effect, as did the modern playwright Samuel Beckett, notably in *Krapp's Last Tape.*

Another function of a play's dialogue is exposition, which refers to the explanation or description of action, events, or people that are not revealed to us directly. So, for example, without even directly showing the fugitive the police are seeking in *The Rising of the Moon,* Lady Gregory, the playwright, informs us what he looks like when the sergeant reads the "wanted" poster. We also learn—without seeing—the fact that the water is close, providing a likely means for escape. What other things does exposition in the dialogue tell you? Unlike short stories and novels, where the narrator can describe events that have happened in the past or make you privy to the thoughts of a character, plays have only dialogue to serve these functions. A good playwright will interweave exposition into what is being said without your being aware of it. One exercise you might try to gain a better sense of the playwright's art is to study the way he or she employs exposition.

As stated before, dialogue is not merely recorded speech, yet critics often speak of a playwright as "having an ear" for dialogue. This usually means that the author seems to have a talent for imitating the tone, the rhythms of speech, and the regional and/or class dialects of the people he is portraying. Thus, while Cutler, Toledo, Slow Drag, and Levee are characters in a play, August Wilson's talent for rendering regional accents, dialect, and slang allows skilled actors to take what these characters say on the page and make it come alive, giving you the impression of real people.

Theme

Theme is as slippery a topic in talking about drama as it is for any genre of literature. For it asks the questions, "What does the play mean?" or "What is the author trying to say?" Understanding the theme or themes of a play seen on a stage may be even more difficult than deciphering the meaning of other forms of literature, since often you will be emotionally carried along by the action, whereas in a novel or short story, you can always pause and consider the significance of what you have read. Although there is no hard and fast rule, it is perhaps in understanding theme that *reading* a play may have an advantage over *seeing* a play.

Sometimes the title of a play can offer a clue to its theme, as do the titles *A Doll's House, A Raisin in the Sun,* and *The Rising of the Moon.* (Note too that the latter two titles have images that have been traditionally used as symbols.) The phrase "a raisin in the sun" is from a poem by Langston Hughes that deplores the betrayal of the promise to provide African Americans with equal rights; the phrase "rising of the moon" suggests an awakening of what is often repressed or suppressed from consciousness, the moon being a symbol in many cultures of the hidden aspect of human nature.

In Hansberry's play, you will find enacted among the characters the fight to achieve racial justice and the outcome of this fight for one family. In Lady Gregory's play, you find the Sergeant's attitude transform from one of an officious civil servant to a humane individual who gets in touch with his early roots and values. Thus *The Rising of the Moon* can be taken to be a statement about the suppression of the Irish independence movement as symbolized through the encounter between the Sergeant and the Ragged Man. The term "doll" as used in doll's house has meanings that go beyond the literal meaning of a child's plaything. In Ibsen's play, Nora seems to be treated as a doll by her husband, and her rebellion at the end is her escape from this unflattering and demeaning role.

Titles aside, themes in plays can be inferred through the study of other images, actions, and statements, particularly when they recur. When you read a play, be aware of such repetitions, and see if there seems to be a common thread that stitches them together. By this method you may be able to interpret motifs in what you read or see to more general or universal pronouncements about the human condition. Critics have noted the importance of Lena Younger's (Mama) plants in *A Raisin in the Sun* and interpret them as symbols for the determined survival of the Younger family. Other critics make much of the tape recorder in *Krapp's Last Tape,* suggesting that it represents the human experience, which is merely a playing out of what has already been recorded by consciousness, providing the dim view that humans have little say in determining their destinies.

To appreciate the full dimension of what you read, and to find hooks that can provide topics for discussion or writing, look for recurring motifs and character transformations in plays. These will more than likely lead you to discovering a play's theme.

INTERPRETING DRAMA

Interpreting plays, like interpreting other works of literature, is an elusive task. You, like your classmates, and readers in general, come to the specific work with your own background, prejudices, viewpoints, and attitudes. In addition, the time you live in, the place you live in, your cultural heritage: all have an impact on the meaning you extract from literature. To give just one superficial example, a salesman, after seeing a performance of Arthur Miller's play *Death of a Salesman*, is reported to have said to his wife, "I always said the Northeast was a lousy sales territory." Whether his pragmatic response to the play was of the sort Miller wanted audience members to have is doubtful; yet, there are *many* possible valid interpretations of a play, not *the* one true interpretation.

Dramatic literature, perhaps more than other forms of literature, should make this indeterminate aspect of interpretation evident, since most plays are meant to be performed. Thus, even the performance of a play will alter the play's import, being influenced by the director's and actors' visions. Another aspect of plays which makes interpretation problematic is the fact that most plays that have lasting appeal are complex works of art, just as is the case with other forms of literature. Therefore, to tease out the meaning from what you read is not as simple as finding the right answer on a multiple choice test. It is rather like deciphering a secret code or putting together the pieces of a puzzle.

Since it is probably impossible to actually *prove* that your interpretation is the right one, it is better to think of interpretation as an argument, that is, as a statement that you will try to back up with evidence from what you have read or seen. And since plays that stand the test of time tend to be complex, it is perhaps better to develop an argument that addresses one aspect of a play rather than the entire play itself. Another reason for limiting your interpretation of a play is that if you select too broad an interpretation, it may be difficult to include all that you need to support your interpretation in a college-length paper. For example, consider the following interpretation of Miller's *Death of a Salesman*: "*Death of a Salesman* shows the tragic consequences of taking at face value the traditional concepts of 'the American dream' without questioning or considering their merits." While this interpretation is valid, it would be nearly impossible to discuss all the pertinent evidence that exists in the play that supports this theme, since the play is replete with images, dialogue, description, and relationships that advance it.

In reading a play carefully, try to find particular speeches, images, symbols, or statements that present a means of interpreting a particular aspect of the play. For example, character is one aspect of a play that deserves special attention, and to which interpretation can bring fruitful results. You may wish to select a character that interests you, intrigues you, or seems to possess a special quality that may be overlooked by a superficial reading of the play. Take for example one student who read August Wilson's play *Ma Rainey's Black Bottom*. Intrigued by the character of Toledo, he reread the text focusing on Toledo's relationships with the other band members, his philosophical statements and observations, and his action during the course of the play. He was particularly intrigued by a speech of his early in Act I:

TOLEDO: See, now . . . I'll tell you something. As long as the colored man look to white folks to put the crown on what he say . . . as long as he looks to white folks for approval . . . then he ain't never gonna find out who he is and what he's about. He's just gonna be about what white folks want him to be about. That's one sure thing.

Reviewing the play, the student then highlighted Toledo's dialogue and found a pattern that seemed to bear out the idea that Toledo was revealing certain truths about the African American's dilemma in America, and that in a sense he becomes a martyr whose truth cannot be accepted by the other members of the band, and thus is killed in the end for his beliefs.

EVALUATING DRAMA

You may interpret the meaning of a play, the significance of a character, the function of setting, and the like, without ever engaging in probably the most common form of writing about drama: evaluating. Theater critics, whether writing for newspapers like *The New York Times,* magazines like *Newsweek,* television news shows, or radio primarily engage in evaluation. That is, while they may describe and summarize a play, their ultimate purpose is to relate to their audiences the quality of the play, whether it is a masterpiece, a terrible travesty of dramatic art, or something in between.

When you evaluate a play, you may not reach a large audience, but you will, at the least, help hone your own critical abilities, and develop for yourself a sense of what makes or does not make for good dramatic literature. Ultimately, evaluation is a subjective affair, but there are certain guidelines that can help you appreciate the quality of a play, whether or not you agree with its message.

The first thing you might do is ask yourself a series of questions that can guide you into understanding why you like or dislike a play. If it moves you emotionally, why? If you identify with the characters, which ones, and why? Even if the world of the play is foreign to you, that is, takes place at another time, in another culture, or among a class of people you are unfamiliar with, ask yourself whether you find any similarities between the world of the characters and the world you yourself have experienced or could imaginatively experience.

Once you've established your own relationship to the play, you have a base from which you may use more abstract criteria in your evaluation. Earlier in this chapter, continuous *action* was described as being an essential part of most drama. Does the action in the play you have read seem coherent and unified? Most students of literature find coherence and unity important characteristics in determining the quality of a work of literature. If a character acts in a way that seems foreign or implausible to his or her nature, the chances are that the playwright has not fleshed out his conception of just who the character is.

Since plays are nearly all dialogue, one important aspect of evaluating a play is the extent to which the dialogue sounds true. Do the characters speak as if they were real people? Can you distinguish their class, culture, age, and personality from the way they speak? Does the dialogue seem to imitate the rhythms of speech? If the answers to these questions are in the negative, they may have a bearing on the quality of the play.

Universality of appeal is another criterion upon which to evaluate a play. Why is it that plays written over 2,000 years ago—for example, *Oedipus Rex* or *Lysistrata*—are still read and performed today? More than likely it is because the issues that these plays raise are still of concern to contemporary audiences. Or take for example plays that seem to cross cultures successfully. *Death of a Salesman* was translated into Chinese and successfully performed in China, a country that does not even have the profession of salesman. Still, audiences found the play pertinent to their lives. Other issues to consider are whether the play presents its world in an interesting, complex, and original fashion. Most people would agree that the world is a complex place with multidimensional challenges. If a play reflects this world, it could hardly do so by being simplistic. Thus, in evaluating a play, another issue to consider is whether the world it depicts addresses the complexity of life. If it lacks this dimension, chances are the play will fade quickly away in your mind whereas a play replete with ideas will be one you can turn to again and again, only to discover more intriguing issues about its characters, meaning, and significance.

Nonetheless, two individuals using all these criteria can come to radically different evaluations about a play, as the following excerpts from reviews of two well-known drama critics reveal. Both were responses to a Lorraine Hansberry (author of *A Raisin in the Sun*) play entitled *Les Blancs*. The first is by John Simon writing in *New York Magazine:*

> . . . The result is unmitigated disaster. *Les Blancs* (the very French title in what is clearly a British African colony testifies to the utter confusion) is not only the worst new play on Broadway, of an amateurishness and crudity unrelieved by its sophomoric stabs at wit, it is also, more detestably, a play finished—or finished off—by white liberals that does its utmost to justify the slaughter of whites by blacks. . . . It is a malodorous, unenlightening mess.

The second is by Walter Kerr, writing for *The New York Times:*

> I urge you to see Lorraine Hansberry's . . . ranging, quick-witted, ruefully savage examination of the state of the African mind today. . . . Virtually all of *Les Blancs* is there on the stage, vivid, stinging, intellectually alive, and what is there is mature work, ready to stand without apology alongside the completed work of our best craftsmen. The language in particular is so unmistakably stage language that . . . it achieves an internal pressure, a demand that you listen to it, that is quite rare on our stages today.

If professional critics can differ so radically in their evaluation of a play, you should rely on your own taste, informed by your growing knowledge of fiction, poetry, and drama, when judging any work of literature.

PART THREE

Writing about Film

CHAPTER 6

Introducing Film:
History and Form

*F*rom its very start in the late nineteenth and early twentieth centuries, filmmaking was a populist art, deriving from the popularity of photography and appealing to people of all classes and backgrounds. In the beginning, small movie theaters called nickelodeons came into being, with very short "moving pictures." People gawked at the sight of phenomena of the real world put on a screen, startled by the sight of a locomotive that seemed about to run over the audience!

Gradually films became longer, and a market developed for movies with more highly evolved stories. This trend developed into the advent of "feature" or full-length films, as we know them today. The United States led the way in film production and distribution, but by the 1920s many other countries, such as France, Italy, Germany, Spain, Russia, and Japan, became well known for producing films that appealed to a wide audience. Today, even in the most remote parts of the world, movies are shown in theaters or on videotape to eager audiences.

An important trend in filmmaking has been the making of so-called classic films. This term often refers to a traditionally Hollywood-made film, where style is subordinated to strong story elements, and the audience is asked to identify with its protagonists. In such films there is a *cause-and-effect* relationship between plot elements, with one event leading to another, as we see a causal relationship between story points. In terms of character behavior, we can see why someone might act in a certain way because those events lead up to that result. In the classic film *The African Queen*, directed by John Huston, we can understand why Rose (Katherine Hepburn) grows to love Charley (Humphrey Bogart) because there are a series of incidents in their relationship that slowly build her appreciation and respect for him. Other classic American films include *Birth of a Nation*, *Mr. Deeds Goes to Town*, *Gone With the Wind*, and *Schindler's List*, while foreign classic films include *The Conformist* (Italy), *The Blue Angel* (Germany), *The Seven Samurai* (Japan), *Lawrence of Arabia* (England), and *Fanny and Alexander* (Sweden). Although admittedly there are many great films in the history of cinema that do not follow this formula, studying the classic film is helpful in learning how to write about cinema. Specifically, we will use one of the most recognized modern classic films, *The Godfather*, directed by Francis Ford Coppola, as a model for photography, writing, acting, and directing.

Film is an art that seems inextricably linked to our perception of the real world, which some define as nature. The noted critic and film theorist Sigfried Kracauer in *Theory of Film* has said that "even the most creative film maker is much less independent of nature in the raw than the painter or poet: that his creativity manifests itself in letting nature in and penetrating it."

The fact that the filmmaker is so tied to nature is one of the fundamental precepts of filmmaking and film criticism. This raises two important questions: What does the filmmaker *do* with the nature that he or she perceives? How *far* does the filmmaker go in trying to manipulate that environment?

A filmmaker in the process of creation is always faced with making numerous choices at every stage of that process. And every choice that is made, whether it be the shot, the framing, the staging, the acting style, or the like, has an effect on the themes and the total look and style of the film, and thus on the subsequent impact of the film on the viewer.

Just as every film has a specific point of view, as audience members we each have a set of experiences that shape our perception of a film. Certain dramatic sequences may touch us because we have had similar experiences. Conversely, there may be a character or element of the film that disturbs us so much that we reject the film totally. How can we reconcile these feelings with the task of writing intelligent analysis? Learning about the elements of film can help us make sound judgments that acknowledge our personal response but also take more objective criteria into consideration.

The elements of film share many similarities with those in the other arts—such as drama, photography, and literature—but there are also significant differences. First of all, film differs from drama in the theater because it is a more concrete medium in terms of the environment. Theater makes greater demands on an audience's imagination. For instance, great Shakespearean theater can take place on the equivalent of a bare stage. In contrast, as Kracauer points out, in film the backgrounds and environments are much more dependent on our perception of the real world and thus are more literal than those in the theater, even in so-called fantasy films where nevertheless every detail is carefully designed for the camera. Also, in theater the staging and technical elements focus the eye, whereas in film the camera movement, shot selection, editing, and framing serve to focus the viewer's attention.

Rene Clair, a famous French director of the 1920s, has stated that "if there is an aesthetics of the cinema . . . it can be summarized in one word: 'movement'." The movement of the camera, unique in the arts, creates a constantly changing image. This establishes the difference between film and photography. Although similar principles apply when it comes to framing, light, and color, the moving image creates a different art form with different rules, diction, and standards.

Film and literature are also fundamentally different mediums with distinct ways of telling stories. Certain elements of literature can be mirrored in film (point of view, story structure, dialogue) but cinema makes totally different demands on the creators and the audience. In a book, for example, one can turn forward or turn back to favorite selections, reviewing a passage again and again, admiring the descriptive power of the language or the idiosyncrasies of a character. But a film has a fixed duration, mirroring one of the conventions of theater, with a beginning, a middle, and an end. (Of course, with DVDs, you can now use the menu to select any film scene for viewing and analysis.) Often a great deal has to be pared from a book if it is to become a successful film. The complexity of character that we can find in a novel has to be conveyed with far fewer words in a film, through very different means: dialogue, staging, and acting. Thus the image we see on the screen has to carry the burden of a message transmitted by the novel through words alone. This is just one of the reasons that it is sometimes difficult for films adapted from literature to be as powerful as their sources.

Film is a commercial enterprise dependent on advanced technology. From film's earliest beginnings, technology has determined the kinds of shots and visual images that are possible. Film stock (the material that is used to photograph the image), cameras, projection equipment, and techniques to produce optical effects all have contributed to molding this art form. Today, computerized work in the field of visual effects as well as the use of advanced digital cameras are changing the character of film and video even as this is being written. So in critiquing film, understanding the technology that is used is crucial to understanding how film affects an audience.

And, of course, all of this technology costs money. A highly expensive studio film like *Titanic* will create certain expectations in an audience primed to see a spectacle bursting with excitement. On the other hand, a low-budget independent film such as *Ulee's Gold*, with Peter Fonda as a reclusive beekeeper, generates quite different expectations. Because of its status as a small independent film, audiences expect to see a character-driven family drama with integrity and originality. In evaluating film, we must take into consideration the type of commercial enterprise it is, and judge accordingly.

Film is above all a collaborative art. There is a school of film criticism, commonly referred to as the "auteur theory," which gives the director predominance above all others involved, but in actuality creative people on a film usually share creative decisions, collaborating regularly in production on key ideas and techniques. The key creators are the screenwriter, the cinematographer, the director, the designers, the composer, and the actors. The success or failure of the film often rests on the integrated accomplishment of these collaborators and their ability to present a unified vision on screen.

THE ELEMENTS OF FILM

Film has its own language and vocabulary. Although many of its key terms—like theme, character, and plot—are familiar to us from literature, they also have significant definitions particular to the film discipline. These elements are discussed in the following sections.

Types of Film

Documentary versus Narrative   The narrative film is a work of fiction. Writers create the dialogue, and actors portray characters who act out their parts on screen in a structured story line. In contrast, the documentary is a form that purports to report on the world as it exists. The documentary filmmaker uses various well-known techniques taken from the world of news reporting: recording events as they happen, recording interviews with participants, and utilizing photographs and testimony of historical figures to portray past events.

Sometimes the distinction between narrative and documentary has to be carefully drawn. For example, occasionally actors are used to portray characters in historical documentaries such as Ken Burns' *Jazz*, usually in voice-over. On the other hand, narrative films will often borrow various documentary techniques: Steve Soderberg in *Traffic* used hand-held cameras and a complicated interweaving of different stories to mimic a documentary "feel." Nevertheless, it is clear that *Traffic* is a narrative film, and *Jazz* is a documentary.

It is generally assumed that documentaries will not deliberately falsify a view of reality. However, it is true that inevitably the documentary will reflect the filmmaker's point of view, resulting in some manipulation of the absolute truth. The main way documentarians shape the story is through choosing the interview subjects, selecting certain shots and framing devices, and most importantly by editing the material to support their vision as filmmakers. To be sure, the director of a documentary may often attempt to show a balanced point of view by posing questions regarding a problem or by advancing various solutions. But often a documentary will abandon such an attempt and use powerful evidence to advance a certain ideological argument, as in the classic Barbara Kopple documentary *Harlan County, USA*, about a miners' strike in Harlan County, Kentucky, in 1973. Here the miners' side in the strike is presented through emotional interviews, songs, meetings, and events on the picket line, while what little we see of the owners' point of view is presented in a negative light. This kind of documentary that presents an argument is called a *rhetorical* form of documentary.

The television show *Sixty Minutes* is a good example of how a rhetorical documentary form can argue a specific point of view. Consider the famous "attack interview" that the show has made famous. In such an interview, we see a person who clearly doesn't want to talk to the camera walking away or covering the lens, reinforcing the audience's perception of the person's guilt. The guilt is assumed even though it has not necessarily been definitively proven. In addition, consider a classic *Sixty Minutes* interview featuring Mike Wallace as he talks to a businessman accused of cheating his customers. The subject is viewed in a tight close-up, revealing tension in his face, while Wallace is seen in medium shot, cool and collected. The ideological point is clear: the subject, on the defensive, is culpable, while Wallace is the calm interrogator. Some of these techniques were widely used in Michael Moore's popular documentary *Roger and Me*.

In evaluating a documentary it is important to understand what kind we are judging and thus what the filmmaker's objectives are. Is the filmmaker trying to put forth his or her own point of view or attempting to show a balanced point of view? What techniques are being used to reveal the point of view? What methods are used to gather data? What are the criteria for choosing the people to be interviewed? What kind of shots are used to portray the subjects, and how does editing contribute to the ideological and emotional effect of the film?

Genre   Film is a popular art, and thus audience expectations often form the basis of critical judgment. If we know, for instance, that a certain kind of movie is advertised as a "horror" film, we expect to be shocked and scared by it. This type of narrative film is called a *genre* film. There are some popular genres with which we are all familiar, such as romantic comedy, action-adventure, science fiction, or character-driven drama. Many films target specific audiences, such as a woman's film or a teenager's film. Even so, many movies today combine traditional ideas of genre. A woman may be the heroine of a thriller *(Lara Croft Tomb Raider);* a Kung Fu movie may also have an African-American comic actor as a star *(Rush Hour).* Such combinations target wider audiences than a genre film normally would.

The most critical principle to remember is that our expectations will have a profound effect on our response as an audience. We will compare a particular thriller film with other thrillers we have seen, and judge accordingly. In evaluating genre, be sure to identify the intended audience of the film. Does the film satisfy expectations of a specific genre? Does the film go beyond expectations and pleasantly surprise us or is it disappointing because it does not fulfill genre expectations?

Theme and Character

Characters are the driving force of film action, just as in drama for the stage and in fiction. And similarly, the screenwriter creates tension through lines by constructing character *objectives* (goals). In *The Godfather,* Michael Corleone's major objective seems to be to protect his family, or as he says, "to be strong for the family just like Papa was." This objective or goal provides much of the dramatic action in the middle and last part of the film since all of his actions relate to this main character objective. Another important principle of screenwriting concerns the element of *conflict,* which is dramatized through the use of *obstacles* that stand in the way of character goals. Again, in *The Godfather,* we see *external* obstacles, such as the other crime families' desire for power, and *internal* ones, such as Michael's struggle to define for himself who he is in terms of his own ethics and values in relation to his family.

Regarding fiction, we have said that it is important for the audience to invest in the characters as people. This is also true in film, where one of the objectives of the screenwriter is to have the audience *identify* with certain characters. Conversely, sometimes, in movies with antiheroes or negative characters, the screenwriter wants the audience to be alienated from them. At any rate, as in drama and fiction, it's important that the characters have depth and unique attributes so that they seem convincing.

In finding the themes of the movie, therefore, it is important to first investigate character. Do we identify with the characters or do they alienate us? Are they convincing as real people? What are the characters' values? Are these values consistent with societal norms or do they go against societal norms? What are the characters' objectives or goals? What are the obstacles that get in the way of those goals? How do the actions of the characters reinforce the themes of the movie? And finally, given our analysis of the characters, what values does the filmmaker want the audience to support or reject?

Point of View

Another important aspect of theme relates to *point of view*. Point of view is a term that has two meanings in film. The first meaning refers to the general point of view of the film: through whose eyes is the story told? Its other meaning describes a specific kind of shot (POV) where the camera takes the viewpoint of one of the characters. Sometimes, when there are no clear narrative signals in a film, the writer analyzing it should look for shots that would help cue the audience to a specific point of view. The three main kinds used in a film narrative are third person (omniscient), first person, and shifting points of view.

The third-person or omniscient narrative is the most familiar to us. It corresponds to the third-person narrative in fiction, where there is an imaginary objective "eye" viewing the events of the story. For example, *The Godfather* is related in omniscient narrative, as various events relating to the family's story occur in a multiplicity of settings with many characters. Sometimes a third-person narrative will resemble the first-person narrative by focusing the story on one character, but some scenes will still be written *without the main character present*. A good example of this is *The Godfather Part II*. Michael Corleone is clearly the central character of this movie, and most of the events of the story are restricted to his range of knowledge, but there are still scenes depicted in which he is not involved. In this way, the film is still defined as a third-person narrative, the most widely used and most conventional point of view in film.

The first-person narrative in film is often signaled by a voice-over, typically following one character's voice through the narrative. In a rare instance, a character will address the camera visually *(Ferris Bueller's Day Off)*. Sometimes the voice-over is used throughout, as in *Affliction*, or as a "framing device" at the beginning and end of a film, as in *American Beauty*. The voice-over helps focus the story on one person, announcing that this character is the center of attention. Often in such a film, all or almost all the events are seen through this person's perspective, someone who is often merely a stand-in for the author.

The shifting point of view is the most interesting narrative technique. Here there may be several narrators, actually seen or used in voice-over. A famous example of this element is Kurosawa's *Rashomon*, which depicts the same story from the point of view of four different characters. In *Pulp Fiction* Quentin Tarantino uses a similar technique without narrators, portraying the same scene at the opening and closing of the film but showing it from the points of view of different characters.

Screenwriting

A writer's role in film is generally more collaborative than it would be in literature or theatre. Often many writers are hired to rework or completely rewrite an original screenplay. Directors and even producers participate in the writing. For example, the screenwriting credit for *The Godfather* reads: "Written by Mario Puzo [writer of the original novel] and Francis Ford Coppola [the director]." Because of the many hands involved in the screenwriting of most films, it's important to look carefully at the credits and research the writing history of a film in order to determine who exactly is responsible for the main part of the writing.

Writers generally write much more sparely for films than for other disciplines, letting the images drive the story. Even in the most literate screenplay, whenever possible, dialogue is often replaced by action. Good screenwriters know that a simple look from one actor to another can transmit a great deal on screen, and they will use such silent moments as part of their writing tools.

Narrative: Plot and Story

The way the story is told is of primary importance in filmmaking, just as it is in literature and drama for the stage. A fundamental distinction in storytelling is the difference between *plot* and *story*. Plot is defined as the ordering of the events that take place during the film as it is presented. Story refers to all the events in a narrative, including ones that are presented as well as those that we infer to have taken place. In *The Godfather*, the narrative of the film concerns a sequence of events spanning a few years that lead to the death of Don Corleone and the ascent of his son Michael to be the next godfather. But there are many events in the past that are referred to in the film that are never seen, such as the story of how Don Corleone first began his life of crime at the turn of the century. When Coppola made *The Godfather Part II*, he filmed many of these story elements that were mentioned but never seen in the first one. We can thus see that *story* in *The Godfather* has turned into *plot elements* in the latter film.

We have already discussed the classic film, where style is subordinated to strong story elements, the audience is asked to identify with its protagonists, and there is a cause-and-effect relationship between plot elements. An important point to add is that although one event leads to another in the classic film, paradoxically there should be surprises and unexpected events that heighten the audience's interest. These surprises and twists are often a sign of good classic filmmaking.

On the other hand, more experimental films will use a *random* or *nonlinear* treatment of story elements. Characters will behave in unexpected ways, without any story preparation for the audience. The events in Fellini's dreamlike *8 1/2* often happen without any logical order or clear effect on Guido, the

main character, but many of these events contribute to the character's alien-
ation, one of the principal thematic elements of that movie. Christopher
Nolan's *Memento* (2001), an interesting twist on the revenge thriller, begins
with the end and ends with a surprise beginning. This backward narrative
technique enhances the audience's surreal experience of following the central
character, a man with severe short-term memory loss, as he pieces together
clues that he—understanding his condition—has left for himself.

Story Structure

Writing a screenplay is all about *structure.* The writer Syd Field and others
have persuasively argued that modern screenplays are usually written with
the *three-act structure* as a basis. This structure uses the elements of the five-
point model of the Aristotelian narrative discussed in the fiction chapter: a beginning and exposition, rising action, the climax, falling action, and resolution.
This structure helps us to understand how film tells a story. Here, then, are the
basic elements of the three-act structure:

> In the first act, the screenwriter introduces the characters, addresses any neces-
> sary exposition, and sets the major conflict into motion. The second act intensi-
> fies this conflict, creating rising action. Often in this act, there are changes or
> shifts in the story that will move the plot into surprising directions. In the third
> act, there is usually a major struggle between the main conflicting forces. This
> action will build to a climax, after which there is falling action and resolution.

Story Structure in Action: A Brief Synopsis of *The Godfather*   The story
structure of *The Godfather* is a good example of the classic form. In the first act,
in the complex wedding sequence, we are introduced to the main characters,
most importantly the Don, Vito Corleone (Marlon Brando). Michael (Al Pa-
cino), the younger son, and his girlfriend, Kay (Diane Keaton), are featured in
a scene in which Michael tells a story about his father's brutal practices and
declares: "That's my family, Kay. It's not me." The next beat of action reveals
both Don Corleone's ruthlessness as well as his loyalty to his family, when he
tries to get his godson, the singer Johnny Fontaine (Al Martino), a part in a
movie. When the producer balks at giving Fontaine the part, the Don has the
producer's favorite horse killed, and the producer finally gives in, granting the
favor to the Don. Now an important plot complication occurs that sets up the
central conflict of the film. The drug king Sollozzo (Al Lettieri) wants to go
into business with the Don and is turned down. The stage is set for a showdown between the two. First, Sollozzo kills the Don's henchman, and then he
tries to assassinate the Don, which brings him near death. This dramatic scene
ends Act I.

The second act escalates the conflict between Sollozzo and the Corleone
family, while laying the groundwork for an important shift in character objective and action for Michael. Despite his initial desire to remain outside the
family "business," Michael is now forced by his loyalty to his father and the
danger of the circumstance to take responsibility and help his family. First,

Michael saves his father from being killed at the hospital, where the Don has been placed after the attempted murder. Now, in the turning point of the film, Michael's character makes a dramatic change when he proposes that he alone will murder Sollozzo and a corrupt police officer. Michael's whole demeanor alters and we see a new Michael, a Michael who is becoming his father, something he implied would never happen. Then, as Michael succeeds in killing Sollozzo and the policeman in the restaurant, the story takes a new turn. A war between all the families ensues. Michael goes to Italy to hide, meets a local girl, and marries her. In New York, as the Don tries to recover, the emotional Santini (James Caan) runs the family in an erratic and impulsive style. His reign ends when he is lured into an ambush at a toll booth and is murdered, leaving a power vacuum at the head of the family. In Italy, Michael's new wife is killed in an assassination attempt on his life, shattering any semblance of peace that Michael had. This marks the end of Act II.

The third act begins with a meeting in which the five families swear peace with each other, a peace that will not hold. Michael returns to New York, marries Kay, and becomes the acting Don with the help of his father and his counsel. Now the final action of the movie commences. Through an elaborate scheme set up by his father and himself, Michael plans to rid the Corleone family of all of their enemies. Although Don Corleone dies before the plan is completed, Michael carries out their plan with coldness and precision. During the baptism of his sister's baby, Michael has his men complete numerous brutal murders, successfully destroying his opposition in the five families and in Las Vegas. He caps this action by ordering the murder of his own brother-in-law for Carlo's past complicity in Santini's murder. He then lies about this murder to his sister and to Kay. His opening statement to Kay, "That's my family. It's not me," can now be seen in ironic contrast to his present actions. The film ends as Kay views a scene reminiscent of the opening of the film, where a supplicant kisses Michael's ring. The door closes on this image, shutting Kay out from the secret life of the family and thereby setting up the future tension between them, one of the major conflicts of the next film in the series (*The Godfather Part II*).

Let us examine how *The Godfather* fits into the classic structure. We can see that indeed the writers use the first act to introduce characters and any necessary story exposition, as well as to begin the action that produces the main conflict or conflicts, in this case (1) Don Corleone versus his enemies (characterized now by Sollozzo) and (2) Michael's internal struggle, caught between his loyalty to his family and his desire to be his own man with his own values. At the end of the act, the Don is nearly killed, laying the groundwork for a major change in direction in the second act. In this act, the conflict between Sollozzo and the Corleone family escalates. Now there is a shift or turn in the plot as Michael decides to take on his father's mantle and "be strong for the family." He commits murder. Problems for the main characters increase and tension rises when the older son, Sonny, is killed, as is Michael's new bride. In Act III we have the showdown between the major forces. Again, there seem to be two major conflicts that now are redefined by circumstances. They are (1) the war against the Corleone enemies, now fought by Michael with his father's help, and (2) Michael's own battle within himself to act honorably or to act completely ruthlessly. In the final showdown, Michael's enemies are killed and he is triumphant. On the other hand, in a moral sense, he seems to have lost the battle with his conscience; he displays a chilling ruthlessness that totally denies the honorable character presented to us in the first scene.

As in all fine works of art, good writing demonstrates unity. Both major conflicts are artfully juggled in all three acts in *The Godfather*, and elements begun in the first act are followed through in the second and resolved in the third.

It should be noted that some films deliberately violate the three-act form, often playing creatively with time and space, as in the aforementioned *Pulp Fiction*, where the first scene is also the last scene in the movie. When encountering a film that deliberately violates these conventions, it's important to notice the similarities and dissimilarities to this form.

In evaluating plot and story structure, ask the following questions: Does the film follow the classic form where there is meant to be a cause-and-effect relationship between plot elements? If so, do these events flow naturally or is there an intrusive authorial presence manipulating these events in a mechanical way? Even though events are prepared for, are there also surprises and twists that help build excitement and hold the audience's interest? Are the characters depicted so that we identify with their goals and problems? Is the central conflict powerful and is there rising action that intensifies the conflict? Has the conflict that is set up in the first act been brought to a resolution in the last act? In more experimental films, do the random plot elements add up to an emotional and/or intellectual effect? If so, how would you describe this effect and how does it relate to the themes of the movie?

Film Adaptation

Adaptation provides particular problems and challenges to the screenwriter. Although films have been adapted from articles, plays, and even comic books *(Superman, Batman)*, the most common adaptation in cinema is from a novel. Films such as *Silence of the Lambs, Remains of the Day, The Wizard of Oz*, and *The Graduate* are all examples of successful film adaptations. As previously noted, adapting a novel will inevitably mean paring down the "canvas" of the book, reducing or eliminating certain subplots, expanding some characters, and eliminating others. It may even involve inventing new ones that may better serve the purpose of telling the story through film. For example, the novelist's view of events may be presented by a specific character, or in some cases his or her attitudes might be portrayed through the use of voice-over.

The adaptation of the film *The Godfather* by Mario Puzo and Francis Ford Coppola from Puzo's novel is a good example of the unique challenges of this sort of adaptation. In the novel *The Godfather*, Mario Puzo attempts an epic form, with in-depth treatment of many characters briefly seen or even eliminated in the movie. Thus in the book we have whole chapters dealing with the inner life and exploits of the singer Johnny Fontaine (the Don's godson), the performer Nino Valenti (his alcoholic friend), Jules Segal (an abortionist doctor in Las Vegas), and Lucy Mancini (a young girl seduced by Sonny Corleone in the opening chapter). These characters are woven through much of the novel and give the story depth and texture that the film does not have. Even some of the important characters of the movie, such as Sonny, Tom Hagen, and Kay, are given much more space in the novel, providing the psychological insight into character that the novelist can portray so skillfully through the technique of lending voice to the person's thoughts through the inner monologue.

As in the novel, the movie's protagonist is Michael Corleone, and there is a strong focus on the Don and his relationship to him. But, as we have seen, the film puts his story much more powerfully in the forefront. Certainly, there are other important characters in the film, but all is subsumed in the effort to let the audience follow Michael's story in depth. His central problem becomes the core of the film's storytelling, and the plot follows his emotional journey, so that his decisions become key in the climax of each act, allowing us as an audience to empathize with him. This technique of reducing the scope of the story and focusing on a few main characters is typical of most film adaptation.

Another difference has to do with structure. Just as in a drama, a film must come to a strong climax, expressed in visual and aural terms. Compare the climax of the book to that of the film. In the novel, the shooting of the Las Vegas mobster Moe Green *precedes* the death of the Godfather and the final shootings in New York by what must be at least a month. The shootings themselves are reported in a dry, minimalist fashion in the book, similar to the style of a newspaper story. In contrast, the screenwriters delay the murder of Moe Green in the film, putting that event together with the other killings of Michael's enemies. As previously noted, this is all realized in one brilliant film sequence that is intercut with Michael's participating in the baptism of his sister's baby, giving the scene an eerie unity. Here, through images and sound, the most sacred moments and the most violent moments of life are juxtaposed in marked contrast to one another, building to a deadly climax.

In conclusion, it's difficult for a film to match a novel in subtlety, depth, and psychological insight. A great film provides something else: a strong story that captures the audience's emotions differently, engaging its eyes and ears in a visceral, powerful way.

You should ask yourself these questions in regard to adaptations: Does the film stand on its own? Can it be fully enjoyed without reading the novel or play upon which it is based? Do the characters and their relationships seem real and compelling or do they seem "literary," stiff, or unlifelike? Do we feel the author's presence in the film through voice-over or embodiment in a character? Is this presence intrusive or does it strengthen and enhance the force of the film?

Elements of Photography in Filmmaking

Just as words make up the diction of literature, shots are the diction of filmmaking. Shots are defined as the images that are recorded continuously from the moment a camera is turned on to the time it is turned off. Describing shots

FIGURE 1   *The Third Man.* A **close-up.**

FIGURE 2   *Fury.* This **high shot** shows us what the hero sees, from his point of view.

involves the concepts of *framing* and *image size.* As in photography, all the information in a shot is contained within the frame. The size of the most important image in a frame (often the human figure) is an element that creates the difference between shots. The noted film authority Louis Gianetti defines them in six basic categories: the extreme long shot, the long shot, the full shot, the medium shot, the close-up, and the extreme close-up.

The *extreme long shot,* often called the *establishing shot,* shows a whole environment of a scene from a distance. Typical examples include a whole building, a street, or a large part of a forest.

The *long shot* presents a character in an important physical context. A typical long shot will show a man in a room, for example, where the shot is wide enough to show the details of the room in relationship to the human subject.

The *full shot* displays exactly what it implies: the full human figure from head to toe.

The *medium shot* reveals the figure from the waist up.

The *close-up* concentrates on the human face or a small object (Figure 1).

The *extreme close-up* is an even "tighter" shot, usually used on the face, and will emphasize elements such as the eyes or mouth.

The *angle* is another important element of film vocabulary; it refers to the camera position of a shot. An *eye-level shot* takes a subject from a normal position and creates a neutral view of it. An *aerial shot,* sometimes called a "bird's eye" shot, shows a view of a scene directly above the subjects. A *high shot* shows a subject from an angle somewhat above it, often tending to diminish that character in terms of power (Figure 2). A *low shot,* taken from below the subject, will tend to increase the power or threatening quality of the subject (Figure 3). For example, low shots have traditionally been used in horror films to arouse fear about a character. A combination of high and low shots edited skillfully in a fight scene may help to build tension and excitement. Finally, there is the *oblique shot,* where the camera is tilted to give an odd, skewed perspective. Spike Lee uses oblique shots in *Do the Right Thing* as part of his

FIGURE 3   *The Maltese Falcon.* This **low shot** of Casper Gutman emphasizes his obesity.
(Casper Gutman: copyright 1949 Warner Brothers)

FIGURE 4   *Do the Right Thing.* An **oblique shot.**
(Spike Lee: Photofest)

filmmaking style to make comments on his characters and the Brooklyn environment of his movie (Figure 4).

As stated, *camera movement* is one of the key elements that distinguishes filmmaking from photography. One of the main examples of camera movement is a *following shot,* which will either *pan* or *track* with a character. A pan is a camera moving laterally on a stationary camera mount such as a tripod, whereas tracking refers to the camera moving on a mobile camera mount in relationship to a subject. An example of a dynamic following shot would be a crane shot tracking an airplane as it takes off.

The *handheld shot* produces the most powerful effect of movement. This is a technique first made popular in documentary films, in which a cameraman abandons the use of a tripod and simply holds the camera, following the movement of the subject. Although the image has much more jarring movement than if fixed on a tripod, this technique has been widely copied for some shots in feature films. The handheld shot produces a feeling of kinetic movement and is associated in the audience's mind with a heightened sense of reality. As previously mentioned, the highly acclaimed film *Traffic* (2001) uses handheld cameras extensively to mimic documentary style and add a sense of gritty realism to its tale about fighting the drug war. A fairly recent invention, the steadicam, takes the technique of handheld camera even further. The camera "floats" in a specially designed rig, allowing the freedom and quick movement of the handheld camera without any jarring movement of the image. Some directors feel that a steadicam shot puts the viewer into the scene in a way that no other shot can.

Lenses and Filters   The use of different lenses is another technique of the camera to change our perceptions. A normal lens—that of 28–40mm—gives a fairly normal image. This is the way most of us see the world. A wide-angle lens, 9–24mm, tends to distort the image, creating more depth of field, so that everything is in focus. It is very useful for long shots where the details of the environment are important. On the other hand, a long lens, 50mm and more, will tend to flatten the image, with only the subject in focus and the rest of the frame out of focus. A long lens is used to eliminate background details, often putting focus on facial expression to highlight an emotional moment in a scene.

Filters are devices (glass or plastic) that, when placed in front of the lens, distort the image in various ways. There are many different kinds of filters: some are used to darken or brighten colors, while some are used for special optical effects, such as light sparkles or soft focus. Different colored filters can create a variety of effects. For example, filters can make a series of shots glow with a sepia tone, imitating the look of old photographs.

Mise-en-Scène

The term "mise-en-scène" refers to the director's staging for the camera. It includes such elements as use of the frame, composition and design, and employment of space. It also refers to the director's use of setting, lighting, costumes, makeup, and acting.

Staging and Composition   The director's staging in film is similar to staging for the stage in that selecting appropriate character behavior becomes the director's main task. The difference in film is that it is staging specifically for the camera. By manipulating images to fit into a frame and making decisions about how exactly to use the camera to shoot the scene, the director can change the scene's very nature.

The main issue for the director is how to *focus* the audience's eye. The composition in the frame will lead the eye to certain images, just as it does in photography. There will be dominant images and those of less importance, all implying thematic meaning. There is also no one formula in composition. Sometimes the eye is drawn to the brightest part of the frame, or sometimes to the tallest image. Sometimes an unusual effect such as a silhouette will help draw the eye.

The *space between the characters* is also significant and conveys important meaning about relationships. In *Citizen Kane,* in the famous breakfast montage, the characters appear to be drawing farther and farther apart, until the last shot shows them at opposite ends of a long table, alienated from one another. Another example can be seen in *The Godfather.* In the first scene between the undertaker and the Don, there is a sense of grave formality: the undertaker stands throughout, separated from the Don by at least three feet, while at the end of the scene he is kissing the Don's hand formally. In a later scene, with Johnny Fontaine, the singer (the Don's godson), the scene is staged quite differently. Johnny is sitting on the Don's desk, near tears, with the Don standing close to him. In contrast to the first scene, we understand the relationship instantly through the director's staging and use of space.

Another important element is closed versus open framing. *Closed framing* means that the frame is artfully constructed so that all the important elements seem to be elegantly portrayed within it; nothing spills out of the frame (Fig-

FIGURE 5   *Touch of Evil.* Depiction of **closed framing.**
(*Touch of Evil:* copyright 1958 Universal)

FIGURE 6   *Greed.* Depiction of **open framing.**

ure 5). *Open framing,* on the other hand, implies that the image wants to spread out of the frame, suggesting more action that the camera does not see (Figure 6). Closed framing denotes more formal composition, while open framing is considered more realistic.

Following is a brief example of student writing that demonstrates an analysis of staging techniques. It concerns a scene from *Eve's Bayou,* directed by Casey Lemmons:

> In the scene outside the party, Eve and her father sit opposite each other in a closed frame on the same level. This shows an intimacy, a lack of fear, and no difference in power between them. It isn't until Eve's mother, Roz, enters that the balance is disrupted. She walks in, framed between them, splitting up their warm two shot. It is clear that the mother is a competitor and breaks the closeness between Louis and all the other women, even her daughter.

Lighting   Lighting helps to create mood, focus our eye, and enhance composition. The contrast between light and shadow is one of the most important elements of film. Highlighting certain parts of the face, such as the eyes, for example, can focus our gaze on the emotions of the character, while darkness can create suspense and a sense of drama.

A realistic technique of lighting uses sources such as the sun, overhead lights, or light through a window to intensify the light in a scene. *Dramatic lighting* will use the principle of source lighting, but it will enhance or extend the effect to create focus and drama in a scene. Usually there are at least two light sources in a scene: a *key light* (the main source) and a *fill light* (a less intense light that helps to fill in shadows, softening the effect).

Lighting needs to be suitable to the themes and tone of a specific film. *High key* is bright and even, using low contrast between brighter and darker areas. It has often been used for comedies, musicals, and certain kinds of epic dramas. *Low key* has traditionally been used for thrillers, mysteries, and dramas where there can be high contrast between light and dark, with a strong use of detailed shadows. In contemporary films, both of these techniques can be used in the same film to produce different effects.

The opening sequence in *The Godfather* is a good example of the use of dramatic lighting for thematic purposes. The film begins with a scene inside a darkened room, where an undertaker is asking the Don for a favor. Using low key lighting, the only light is on the faces of the characters; the scene appears to be taking place against a virtual dark background (Figure 7). The faces seem almost to be floating in space, disembodied from their environment. The one exception is a shot where Brando's face is silhouetted against the bright pattern of the lights striking the blinds in the window, creating a sense of mystery. This dark interior scene is contrasted with the sequence of a bright wedding scene outside (Figure 8), shot in high key. The meaning is clear: there is a disparity between what goes on in the light and what goes on in the dark. The theme of hidden, dark power has already been communicated just through the medium of lighting.

Sets, Costumes, and Makeup   Setting is of predominant importance in film. Just as in staging, placing a camera in front of a setting changes its nature because of framing. How that environment is seen transmits important thematic messages. Similar to drama on stage, a setting communicates detail about the characters—how they live, what is important to them, and so on. The austere castle of *Citizen Kane* communicates coldness and pretension; this is in contrast to the warm interiors of a film such as *Hannah and Her Sisters* or the apartment scenes of the young Corleone family in *The Godfather Part II*. Many set decorators believe that their most important task is deciding what to *remove* from a naturalistic environment. The selection of a few telling elements in set decoration—a photo of a loved one, or the frayed pillow on a couch—can often communicate important story points more effectively than the use of a multiplicity of random elements.

Many sets in film attempt to imitate life: they are "found" on location (a street in New York, for example) or constructed to imitate life, either in a studio environment or on location. But in contrast to the realistic approach, sometimes sets are highly stylized, as in the expressionist film *The Cabinet of Dr. Caligari* or the frightening hotel hallways of *The Shining*. These theatrical settings give an appropriate context for the characters' odd behavior in a stylized film.

Costumes and makeup become one of many tools to reveal character and reinforce the film's themes. A costume can place a character in a certain historical period as well as in a social or economic class. In addition, it can help reveal character traits and become integral to an audience's perception of a character "image"—think of Batman's cape or Stanley's torn T-shirt in *A Streetcar Named Desire*. Costumes can be very realistic or can veer toward stylization with symbolic meaning (Fellini's *Juliet of the Spirits*). Makeup for realistic films is generally subtler than makeup for stage, although it is as important in revealing character through certain hairstyles and cosmetics. Wigs and false noses can be more significant in stylized and nonrealistic films. Consider Olivier's makeup

(*Godfather:* Photofest)

FIGURE 7 & 8   *The Godfather.* In Fig. 7, **low-key** lighting sets the mood for the dark interior dealings between the undertaker and the Don. The following scene—the bright wedding in Fig. 8—is shot in **high key.** These contrasts in lighting emphasize the disparity between the bright, open future Michael promises his wife and the dark, hidden power of his family.
(*Godfather:* Photofest)

in *Richard III* or Orson Welles' makeup in *Citizen Kane*. In science fiction and fantasy films such as *Planet of the Apes*, costumes and makeup can become the most important design elements in the film.

Color   Since the 1930s, color has become one of the key components of all design in the use of filters, lighting, sets, costumes, and makeup. Often, of course, color is used realistically to satisfy audience expectations, especially in settings and costumes. On the other hand, saturated color can be used with any one of these elements to produce a rich, theatrical effect, as in a Fellini film like *Casanova* or the musical *Moulin Rouge*. A designer will often use what is termed a "limited palette" of just a few colors to produce specific effects. An extreme example is using just whites, blacks, and grays, as in George Lucas' science fiction movie *THX 1138*. And sometimes one color is used predominantly, such as red, which can be symbolic of romance or terror.

Of course, films used to be shot in black and white until the onset of advanced color techniques. Today, it is a bold choice to shoot in black and white, and usually reveals ambitious artistic intentions. Spielberg made this choice in filming *Schindler's List*, although he used color sparingly by portraying a mysterious girl in a red dress for symbolic effect.

Following is a brief excerpt of student writing that describes how color can be used to underscore thematic meaning in *Do the Right Thing*:

> The overwhelming use of red in the film in these early scenes is a prelude to the imminent violence that would explode on screen. The color appears in nearly every outdoor scene but is especially focal when serving as the backdrop for the corner where Sweet Dick Willie and his cohorts congregate . . . Extreme close-ups reveal faces and bodies beaded by sweat. The red background seems appropriate as the three men appear to be steaming on a red-hot griddle. The red also may serve as a sign of the bloodshed that is hopelessly unavoidable, a harbinger of things to come.

Acting   "If you catch somebody 'acting' in a movie," writes the famous British actor Michael Caine in *Acting in Film*, "that actor is doing it wrong. The moment he's caught 'performing' for the camera, the actor has blown his cover . . . If your concentration is total and your performance is truthful, you can lean back and the camera will catch you every time, it will never let you fall."

Acting in film is a discipline that is strikingly different from acting on stage. While in theater an actor has to project his or her emotions across the proscenium, a camera in close-up records every minute detail of the character's thoughts and emotions. As Michael Caine implies in the above quote, relaxation is one of the most essential elements of acting for film; those actors who are most relaxed are often the most believable as well as the most successful. Critics will say of such actors that the camera "loves" them. Great actors in realistic films give concrete examples of specially observed reality to convince us of the truthfulness of their performance. Think of Dustin Hoffman's strangely inflected speech in *Rain Man* or Diane Keaton's nervous mannerisms in *Annie Hall*. Sometimes an actor in film will even use technical and artificial elements you would normally see on stage and meld them with a convincing film performance. Marlon Brando used a great many technical elements (prosthetics for his mouth and a stylized way of speaking) to produce a very theatrical character in *The Godfather,* but he combined these technical elements with well-observed character idiosyncrasies and emotional veracity. In every frame, Brando conveys what the great acting teacher Stanislavsky called the "inner truth" of the character.

It should also be noted that for some films the acting is broad and stylized as, for example, in a farcical comedy, a science-fiction movie, or a musical. You must be sure to note the genre when evaluating a specific performance.

In evaluating acting in film, we must ask: Does the actor convince us that he or she is this character? What behavioral details make the performance convincing? If the performance is not convincing, why not? Can you catch the actor "acting" or pushing too hard to perform? Is the acting style appropriate for the specific film genre? If the performance is stylized in some ways, are there still elements that enable you to believe in the basic truth of the character?

Below is a writing sample analyzing elements of photography as well as mise-en-scène. It focuses on a scene between Radio Raheem and a group of Puerto Ricans in Spike Lee's *Do the Right Thing.* Note how concrete details of photography and mise-en-scène (including acting) are linked to thematic issues.

> The scene begins with a shot of the Puerto Ricans talking together, listening to their salsa music. Then Radio Raheem comes into the scene with his radio blasting his trademark song: "Fight the Power." In a medium shot, we see Stevie, one of the Puerto Ricans, turning up the volume of his radio, while the camera pans to reveal Radio Raheem lift his larger radio to fill almost a third of the frame, turning up his volume as well. The camera pans back and forth between them until Stevie concedes defeat with a rueful expression, turning his radio down. The scene ends with a long high shot of the street as Radio Raheem walks away, his back to the camera, leaving the shouting Puerto Ricans behind. A small African-American boy runs after him, and he and Raheem share a high five as Raheem raises his arm in triumph.
>
> It's important to notice how theatrical the scene is, almost posed for effect, which tends to distance us and let us observe the scene for humor rather than draw us into the potential danger of the scene. This is achieved through framing, the use of pans, the acting, and finally by the angle and lens of the final shot.
>
> At the beginning of the sequence, the Puerto Ricans are seen in a classical composition of closed form in framing, reinforcing their sense of solidarity but also revealing that the scene has been carefully staged. Indeed all the shots in the scene reflect this kind of conscious framing. In addition, Spike Lee's use of panning is also theatrical and playful, setting up the macho war of the boom boxes. A cut can imply a separation, tension, and would seem useful in such a scene, but in this case Lee uses pans to tie both Raheem and Stevie together. When Raheem's box starts to fill the frame, as if to say, "mine is bigger than yours," we are eager to see Stevie's reaction. The timing of the slow pan back to Stevie creates a further sense of expectation and fun in the scene.
>
> When the camera comes to Stevie, he shows deference to Raheem in a medium close-up, and a slight smile begins to form on his lips. Through this

actor's performance, we feel that Stevie acknowledges Raheem's power. And it seems that Raheem gains strength from that look and from his "win." He raises his arm in the air and actually seems for a moment to become a role model for this small child. This image is all the more poignant because it is one of the few times that there is any kind of black victory in this film. It has added significance because Lee utilizes a wide-angle shot reminiscent of the first shot of the narrative, the high view of this neighborhood. The shot seems to exult in the black triumph, telling us "this is our neighborhood, now see how powerful we are."

In context with the rest of the movie, this scene reveals that it is possible to have battles without bloodshed. The pans especially reinforce the feeling that the blacks and Puerto Ricans are of the same neighborhood, of a similar lifestyle, and that they are connected to each other. Today one may win and one may lose, but life will go on and no one will get hurt.

Sound

Sound is an often unheralded part of filmmaking that can affect our response without our conscious knowledge. Through the details of natural and artificial aural effects, sound helps us to identify more strongly with the fictional situation on screen.

Remember that the early "motion pictures" were just that—moving images without sound. In these early motion pictures, there was often printed dialogue at the bottom of the frame or on a separate frame. What was missing was sound. It wasn't until 1927 that sound could be heard briefly in a film, *The Jazz Singer*, starring Al Jolson. It was released at precisely the time that American jazz was beginning to captivate the world, and from *The Jazz Singer* came Jolson's famous, boastful prediction, "You ain't seen nuthin' yet!"

The sound technique we are most familiar with is live sound, which is recorded at the moment the camera is rolling. This is also called *synchronous sound,* since the object is to synchronize the dialogue and effects (such as knocking on a door) with all the visuals.

However skillful the recording is, filmmakers also use added sound effects after shooting, in what is called *postproduction.* A beach scene where a couple walks across the sand filled with shells, sounds of seagulls and/or children playing may be added in a studio, even though these elements weren't part of the original sound environment. In addition, the sound of walking through sand and shells may be "foleyed," meaning that a sound effects technician makes the effect afterward, precisely matching the visual. All these extra effects create a rich texture of sound, helping the audience become totally immersed in the reality of the scene.

Sometimes sound is created in the studio to produce nonrealistic effects, as in the frightening noises produced by the girl in *The Exorcist,* or the heartbeat used as background for a dream sequence in Bergman's *Wild Strawberries.* Such sounds add unforgettable emotional power to these sequences.

Of course, music can be equally important to a film. It may help create a mood, build tension, or remind us of a time, place, or person. Music is often used thematically; that is, certain themes or melodies may be associated with certain characters or emotional states. When these themes return, they help an audience associate the image with that feeling. In *The Godfather*, the major theme by Nino Rota is almost sentimental in the way it harkens back to the Italian roots of the family. When it is used in different scenes, even in violent ones, the audience is reminded of the emotional connections within the family.

A skillful use of both music and sound in *The Godfather* is the scene where the movie producer discovers the severed horse head in his bed. The sequence starts in virtual silence, with several dissolves of the exterior of the mansion, as the camera pulls us in closer and closer. Now the familiar main theme music of the film sneaks in softly. Then, when we see the producer sleeping in bed, the theme moves into a "B" section with a variation that sounds like calliope music for a carousel. At first playful, this music gradually becomes more and more dissonant and rises in volume and intensity, climaxing the moment when the producer finds the bloody head. At the climax of the music, he begins to scream as the music stops. But his screams continue on and on—then silence. Sound and music have combined to produce a chilling effect.

Here are some important questions for analysis of sound and music: Is synchronous and postproduction sound used for realistic purposes, or is it used to create certain nonrealistic effects? What sounds seem especially important in heightening important moments in the film? Can you identify the musical themes of the movie? Do these themes have any connection to the film's general themes? How does music and sound make certain sequences effective?

Editing

Editing is integral to the way that film tells the story. The word "cut" is familiarly used in editing, defining the basic technique. Just as in a computer word-processing program, the editor cuts and pastes together shots from a film, selecting the information from the scenes to be seen and assembled. Since the days of D. W. Griffith in the early twentieth century, editing has produced a powerful effect on the organization and structure of a film.

Some basic terms of editing are useful to know as a tool for analysis. Remember that a shot is defined as the images that are recorded continuously from when a camera is started until it is turned off. Even so, an editor will usually cut into this shot in order to move on to another. Therefore, a *cut* or edit terminates one shot and begins the next. Sometimes, instead of a "hard" cut, a *dissolve* is used, superimposing one shot over another briefly before the other shot takes over. *Fade ins* (usually from black) and *fade outs* (usually to black) are used to gradually begin images or gradually terminate them.

Frequently in editing, sound and music are used in tandem to bridge cuts and make them smoother. It is also used as a contrasting element to give the shots added meaning. In some of the great battle scenes in Kurosawa's *Ran*, however, all natural sound is cut out completely and symphonic music takes over, creating a dreamlike effect, heightened by the use of slow motion.

The conventional editing technique is called *continuity editing*, where an action sequence is cut so that each part seems to be continuous in time. Here is an example: a man reaches for the doorway in long shot, cut to the hand on the door, cut to the door opening in medium shot, and then cut to a reverse shot of the man walking through the door. In such editing, the editor's input is virtually invisible, and the action seems to take place seamlessly in real time. But, if one wants to jolt the audience by an odd or unique succession of images, the *jump cut* is used instead. Here, the editor will remove elements that help continuity, cutting, for example, from a man walking to a closed door to him walking away from the now open door.

Another kind of editing is *associative editing*. This is when certain images are placed together not in a logical sequence but one in which the juxtaposition of the images has significance. The association of the images creates a new meaning, more than the sum of all the shots together. Such juxtaposition is often used in nonrealistic sequences. Intercutting two or more kinds of sequences is an outgrowth of such technique. Think of the climax of *The Godfather*, which intercuts the baptism of a child with the brutal murders of Michael Corleone's enemies. Sound makes the sequence even more powerful; the soft murmuring of the catechism of the baptismal service is used both to bridge edits and as a contrasting element, as the scenes move back and forth between the baptism and the murders.

Rhythm and pace are other important elements of editing. In a climactic sequence, an editor may break the shots into shorter and shorter units, heightening the tension of a film as it moves toward a climax.

Sometimes filmmakers want to make a story point visually, without dialogue, using a combination of music and sound to help demarcate the passage of time. For example, a sequence will show a couple falling in love in a succession of romantic encounters, rather than dialogue scenes. Such a sequence is called a *montage.*

In analyzing a certain sequence in terms of editing, you might ask yourself these questions: Do the shots seem long in duration, or does the editor try to break the shots of a sequence into short units? Does the rhythm of editing change as a sequence progresses? Does this help create tension or further the action? Is music or sound used in interesting ways to make the edits work better? Are dissolves used instead of "hard" cuts? What is their effect on the storytelling? Is the editing mainly continuity editing or are there sequences where jump cuts and/or associative editing is used? If images are juxtaposed with each other, what is their meaning? Are some of these images being used as symbols? How does the editing style affect an audience and relate to the themes of the movie?

Below is a writing sample that emphasizes editing in a montage sequence in *Eve's Bayou,* directed by Casey Lemmons:

> When Eve has her first premonition in the film, we get an interesting mixture of formal and expressionistic movie-making technique. Eve falls asleep and foresees the death of her uncle, who gets killed in a car accident on the way

home. In her premonition we see flashes, a spider, a coin, a falling hat, and her uncle's car. Overexposure is used to flash from shot to shot in a quick cutting montage style. We also see repetition of past events such as Eve watching her drunken uncle leave in his car, which is driven by his wife, Mozzette. Thus, past and future intermingle, until Eve wakes up in the present, startled by her vision of death. There is a mixture of temporal ellipsis and associative editing, as past events are relived, and images appear which in and of themselves would have no connection to the plot, the characters, or the "reality" of the film. . . . They are effective, however, because they serve the purpose of making a psychological connection to the characters and events about to unfold. These images also convey the emotional and psychological state of the characters and even speak to the themes of the movie. The spider's web, for example, reinforces the concept of memory being a tapestry. The premonition sequences are shot in black and white, in contrast to the rest of the film, which further adds to the tapestry theme and mystic ambiance of *Eve's Bayou.*

INTERPRETING FILM

Robert Corrigan has identified several different approaches in critiquing film. The most important approaches are *auteur, historical, genre, ideological,* and *formalistic.* As mentioned in the introduction to this chapter, the *auteur theory* looks at a film from the standpoint of the major creative force, usually the director. This theory implies that there are common qualities or stylistic devices in any director's body of work. For instance, certain films of a director can be compared to each other, or one director's work can be compared to another's.

Another common approach is the *historical* one, whereby the film's historical context becomes the most important factor in criticism. Here the writer can look at film practices of the period, compare and contrast other films of that period, or compare films of different periods. Then there is *genre criticism,* already discussed, which links films with similar styles, themes, and narratives into a specific group such as horror, westerns, thrillers, teenage comedy, and so forth. In this instance, the film under study is usually compared to other films of that genre. In *ideological criticism,* the writer evaluates what the film is trying to say in terms of its political message, often comparing it to other films or works of that ideology. A film may state its message so explicitly that the film may seem like propaganda (Oliver Stone's *JFK*), or the film's ideology may be more subtle, implying certain cultural and political value judgments without overtly stating them (Garry Marshall's *Pretty Woman*). Uncovering and evaluating a film's ideological message can be one of the most interesting and fruitful tasks in film criticism.

Finally, *formalistic criticism* focuses on certain specific elements of film discussed in this chapter, such as mise-en-scène, camera techniques, or narrative devices. Usually a writer will choose one or sometimes a combination of two of these approaches in a critique of film.

EVALUATING FILM

In evaluating whether a film is "good" or not, it is important to consider a few main points that will aid in writing a critical overview. First, there is the question of unity of style. Do the most important filmic elements such as photography, acting, editing, and design support and complement each other? Is this unified style supportive of a strong theme? Does the film fit into a certain genre? Does it imaginatively add something to the traditions of that genre or does it merely copy them in a clichéd manner?

Second, there is the film's structure and script. If the film follows the classic form, is there a cause-and-effect relationship between elements? Do events flow naturally, and in this flow of action are there surprises and twists that engage an audience's interest? Are the story elements chosen carefully so that plot elements introduced in the first act come to fruition in the second and third? Is there a strong climax and resolution? If the structure is nonlinear, do these varied elements build to some powerful emotional and/or intellectual effect? Does the dialogue seem appropriate to the style and environment of the film? If it is meant to be a realistic film, is the dialogue natural and spontaneous?

Third, we must examine the issue of character and acting. Do the characters and relationships seem specific and real? Do we identify with their goals and problems? Do the actors seem convincing? Do the actors present well-observed character details? Is there emotional truth in the playing? Is the acting style appropriate for the specific film genre?

Finally, we need to look at a film as a whole. Common-sense issues are certainly relevant. For example, does the film hold our interest throughout? Also, do we care about what happens on the screen? And after we leave the theater, has the film had a powerful effect on us? The answer to this last question separates the great films from the merely good ones.

The well-known theater and film director Peter Brook, in his important book *The Empty Space,* analyzes this kind of effect on an audience. Even though he is writing about the theater, his remarks are also applicable to the art of film:

> I know of one acid test . . . When a performance is over, what remains? . . .
> The event scorches on to the memory an outline, a taste, a trace, a smell—a picture. It is the . . . central image that remains, its silhouette, and if the elements are rightly blended this silhouette will be its meaning, this shape will be the essence of what it has to say . . . A few hours could amend my thinking for life. This is almost but not quite impossible to achieve.

Thus, according to Brook, we might ask two questions: Does the film engage our imaginations to such an extent that the images, dialogue, or sounds "scorch . . . our memory?" Has the experience of watching the film made us think or feel differently than we did before?

The following review of *Rocky* by the respected late critic Pauline Kael is a good illustration of a cogent analysis of film. Note that she only chooses a few elements to evaluate in depth, and she makes this analysis with strong arguments based on specific observation and telling examples. To appreciate Kael's essay as a model of film criticism, consider these questions: What does Kael presuppose about her audience? How do the opening and closing paragraphs of Kael's essay complement each other? What is the overall structure of her review? What are the focal points of each paragraph and what modes of paragraph development does she use? How do her knowledge of film culture and her descriptive powers reinforce her central meanings?

Pauline Kael Review of *Rocky*

Chunky, muscle-bound Sylvester Stallone looks repulsive one moment, noble the next, and sometimes both at once. In *Rocky*, which he wrote and stars in, he's a thirty-year-old club fighter who works as a strong-arm man, collecting money for a loan shark. Rocky never got anywhere, and he has nothing; he lives in a Philadelphia tenement, and even the name he fights under—the Italian Stallion—has become a joke. But the world heavyweight champion, Apollo Creed (Carl Weathers), who's a smart black jester, like Muhammad Ali, announces that for his Bicentennial New Year's fight he'll give an unknown a shot at the title, and he picks the Italian Stallion for the racial-sexual overtones of the contest. This small romantic fable is about a palooka gaining his manhood; it's Terry Malloy finally getting his chance to be somebody. *Rocky* is a threadbare patchwork of old-movie bits (*On the Waterfront, Marty, Somebody Up There Likes Me,* Capra's *Meet John Doe,* and maybe even a little of Preston Sturges' *Hail the Conquering Hero*), yet it's engaging, and the naïve elements are emotionally effective. John G. Avildsen's directing is his usual strictly-from-hunger approach; he slams through a picture like a poor man's Sidney Lumet. But a more painstaking director would have been too proud to shoot the mildewed ideas and would have tried to throw out as many as possible and to conceal the others—and would probably have wrecked the movie. *Rocky* is shameless, and that's why—on a certain level—it works. What holds it together is innocence.

In his offscreen bravado, Stallone (in Italian *stallone* means stallion) has claimed that he wrote the script in three and a half days, and some professional screenwriters, seeing what a ragtag of a script it is, may think that they could have done it in two and a half. But they wouldn't have been able to believe in what they did, and it wouldn't have got the audience cheering, the way *Rocky* does. The innocence that makes this picture so winning emanates from Sylvester Stallone. It's a street-wise, flowers-blooming-in-the-garbage innocence. Stallone plays a waif, a strong-arm man who doesn't want to hurt anybody, a loner with only his pet turtles to talk to. Yet the character doesn't come across as maudlin. Stallone looks like a big, battered Paul McCartney. There's bullnecked energy in him, smoldering; he has a field of force, like Brando's. And he knows how to use his overripe, cartoon sensuality—the eyelids at half-mast, the sad brown eyes and twisted, hurt mouth. Victor Mature also had this thick sensuality, but the movies used him as if it were simply plushy handsomeness, and so he became ridiculous, until he learned—too late—to act. Stallone is aware that we see him as a hulk, and he plays against this comically and tenderly. In his deep, caveman's voice, he gives the most surprising, sharp, fresh shadings to his lines. He's at his funniest trying to explain to his boss why he didn't break somebody's thumbs, as he'd been told to; he's even funny talking to his turtles. He pulls the whiskers off the film's cliché situations, so that we're constantly charmed by him, waiting for what he'll say next. He's like a child who never ceases to amaze us.

Stallone has the gift of direct communication with the audience. Rocky's naïve observations come from so deep inside him that they have a Lewis Carroll enchantment. His unworldliness makes him seem dumb, but we know better; we understand what he feels at every moment. Rocky is the embodiment of the out-of-fashion pure-at-heart. His macho strut belongs with the ducktails of the fifties—he's a sagging peacock. I'm not sure how much of his archaism is thought out, how much is the accidental result of Stallone's overdeveloped, weight lifter's muscles combined with his simplistic beliefs, but Rocky represents the redemption of an earlier ideal—the man as rock for woman to cleave to. Talia Shire plays Adrian, a shy girl with glasses who works in a pet store; she's the Betsy Blair to Stallone's Marty. It's unspeakably musty, but they put it over; her delicacy (that of a button-faced Audrey Hepburn) is the right counterpoint to his primitivism. It's clear that he's drawn to her because she isn't fast or rough and doesn't make fun of him; she doesn't make hostile wisecracks, like the kids in the street. We don't groan at this, because he's such a *tortured* macho nice-guy—he has failed his own high ideals. And who doesn't have a soft spot for the teen-age aspirations congealed inside this thirty-year-old bum?

Stallone is the picture, but the performers who revolve around him are talented. Carl Weathers, a former Oakland Raiders linebacker, is a real find. His Apollo Creed has the flash and ebullience to put the fairy-tale plot in motion; when the champ arrives at the ring dressed as Uncle Sam, no one could enjoy the racial joke as much as he does. Adrian's heavyset brother Paulie is played by Burt Young, who has been turning up in movies more and more frequently in the past three years and still gives the impression that his abilities haven't begun to be tapped. Young, who actually was a professional fighter, has the cracked, mottled voice of someone who's taken a lot of punishment in the sinuses; the resonance is gone. As Mickey, the ancient pug who runs a fighter's gym, Burgess Meredith uses the harsh, racking sound of a man who's been punched too often in the vocal cords. The director overemphasizes Meredith's performance (much as John Schlesinger did in *The Day of the Locust*); Meredith would look better if we were left to discover how good he is for ourselves. I found *Marty* dreary, because the people in it were sapped of energy. But Stallone and Talia Shire and the others here have a restrained force; you feel that they're being pressed down, that they're under a lid. The only one who gets a chance to explode is Paulie, when, in a rage, he wields a baseball bat, and it's a poor scene, out of tune. Yet the actors themselves have so much more to them than they're using that what comes across in their performances is what's under the lid. The actors—and this includes Joe Spinell as Gazzo, Rocky's gangster boss—enable us to feel their reserves of intelligence; they provide tact and taste, which aren't in long supply in an Avildsen film.

Rocky is the kind of movie in which the shots are underlighted, because the characters are poor and it's wintertime. I was almost never convinced that the camera was in the right place. The shots don't match well, and they're put together jerkily, with cheap romantic music thrown in like cement blocks of lyricism, and sheer noise used to build up excitement at the climactic prizefight, where the camera is so close to the fighters that you can't feel the rhythm of the encounter. And the film doesn't follow through on what it prepares. Early on, we see Rocky with the street-corner kids in his skid-row neighborhood, but we never get to see how these kids react to his training or to the fight itself. Even the bull mastiff who keeps Rocky company on his early-morning runs is lost track of. I get the feeling that Avildsen is so impatient to finish a film on schedule (or before, as if it were a race) that he hardly bothers to think it out. I hate the way *Rocky* is made, yet better might be worse in this case. Unless a director could take this material and transform it into sentimental urban poetry—a modern equivalent of what Frank Borzage used to do in pictures such as *Man's Castle,* with Spencer Tracy and Loretta Young—we're probably better off with Avildsen's sloppiness than with careful planning; a craftsmanlike *Rocky* would be obsolete, like a TV play of the fifties.

Stallone can certainly write; that is, he can write scenes and dialogue. But as a writer he stays inside the character; we never get a clear outside view of Rocky. For that, Stallone falls back on clichés, on an urban-primitive myth: at the end, Rocky has everything a man needs—his manhood, his woman, maybe even his dog. (If it were rural-primitive, he'd have some land, too.) In a sense, *Rocky* is a piece of innocent art, but its innocence doesn't sit too well. The bad side of *Rocky* is its resemblance to *Marty*—its folklorish, grubby littleness. Unpretentiousness shouldn't be used as a virtue. This warmed-over bum-into-man myth is unworthy of the freak macho force of its star; talking to turtles is too endearing. What separates Stallone from a Brando is that everything Stallone does has one purpose: to make you like him. He may not know how good he could be if he'd stop snuggling into your heart. If not—well, he may be to acting what Mario Lanza was to singing, and that's a form of bumminess.

PRACTICAL SUGGESTIONS FOR WRITING

When writing about film, there are certain guidelines that may be helpful in producing intelligent and sensitive analyses. You might think of them as steps in your prewriting process:

1. **See a film more than once.** It's very difficult to evaluate and analyze a film after only one viewing. As you see it again, your response may change, or conversely, a re-viewing may help validate your response and find examples to confirm your ideas. If the film is available on video or DVD, get a copy so you can review particular sequences at will.
2. **Use note-taking techniques.** When re-viewing, focus on those sequences you want to write about, using shorthand to note elements such as shots, staging, framing, sets, lighting, editing, and acting. Then when you write, you can be specific in describing a scene or sequences.
3. **Try to uncover the theme of the film.** One of your first tasks is to determine what the filmmaker is trying to say. After viewing the film once or several times, analyze the major elements with the theme in mind, focusing in particular on point of view, character values and objectives, and plot. What clues do they give to the theme of the movie? An additional

strategy in determining theme is to focus on the beginning and end of the movie. Are there certain similar thematic elements in these sequences that relate to the larger story elements of the film? For example, it has been noted that the opening of *The Godfather* concerns secret requests in a dark room and ends with a door closing on a similar ritual, shutting out Michael's wife, Kay. These images are connected and have particular relevance to theme. So when you look at the beginning and ending of the film you are studying, you might ask yourself what images and symbols seem important to the filmmaker, and try to penetrate their meaning. It might help at this point to draft your version of the film's theme to aid you in the rest of your writing.

4. **Determine your point of view.** What do you want to say about the film? You may have an emotional response to the film as well as an intellectual one. Try to evaluate both kinds of responses on the basis of what you know about film technique and style, then choose what you most want to communicate to others about the work. Note that you may not be able to decide on your thesis immediately, so give yourself time and jot down several ideas that might become your thesis.

    It's often helpful to compare the film you are critiquing to something else, either the source material (a novel or a play) or another film. But what kind of comparison are you going to make? In choosing which approach to use (historical, genre, etc.), try to decide which one is the most appropriate in communicating your thesis. For example, if the political and social values of *The Godfather* are the most powerful elements for you, you will take the ideological approach and select and analyze these elements from the film that most strongly convey ideology.

5. **Focus on a few elements.** Once you understand the basic concepts of screenwriting and filmmaking, it is tempting to write about everything you notice in a film, from screenwriting to mise-en-scène to camera angles. *Resist this temptation.* The more narrow your focus, the more you will be able to write specifically and persuasively. *Please focus on a few elements that will best illustrate your thesis.*

6. **Focus on a few scenes or sequences.** Just as it's inadvisable to analyze all the elements of a film in one paper, try to avoid mentioning all the scenes that interest you. Unless your criticism focuses on the entire plot, just pick a few scenes or sequences to analyze in depth, and you will have a much better essay.

7. **Use specific examples.** When you analyze an element in a film, whether it is a shot, a line of dialogue, a camera angle, or an actor's behavior, you need to describe this element with as much concrete detail as possible. In describing a shot, for example, you may first want to label it, then describe it further: What is the angle? What kind of camera movement is involved? Exactly what is the framing? Describe what is most important in the composition of the frame. If you are describing an actor's behavior in a scene, try to be as specific as possible regarding the actor's attitude, gestures, fa-

cial expression, and the like. These specific details will constitute the hard evidence that will prove your thesis.

8. **Relate technique to theme and story.** Remember that there is always a purpose to a director's staging or the angle of a specific shot. How does your example fit into the larger meaning of the film?

Siegfried Kracauer has said, "The cinema . . . aims at transforming the agitated witness into a conscious observer." In other words, although the images on the screen may upset and/or move us, our knowledge of the elements of film help us to be aware not only of what we are feeling but also what on the screen causes such responses. First we need to validate our response: Is this feeling so personal that others could not share it? Or are there reasons and evidence based on what we know about film that give our response credibility? Finding out *why* we feel something and then supporting that feeling with concrete evidence will produce the most effective criticism. And in the process of researching the elements of a particular film and analyzing these elements, we may even discover that our response can change. The act of writing can deepen our understanding not only of film, but also of ourselves.

PART FOUR

A Guide to Research and Documentation

CHAPTER 7

Writing Research Papers

A research paper is a report in which you synthesize information on your topic, contributing your own analysis and evaluation to the subject. Research writing is a form of problem solving. You identify a problem, form a hypothesis (an unproven thesis, theory, or argument), gather and organize information from various sources, assess and interpret data, evaluate alternatives, reach conclusions, and provide documentation.

Research writing is both exciting and demanding. American essayist and novelist Joan Didion states, "The element of discovery takes place, in nonfiction, not during the writing but during the research." Nowhere is the interplay of the stages in the composing process more evident than in writing research papers. Prewriting is an especially important stage, for the bulk of your research and bibliographical spadework is done before you actually sit down to draft your report. Moreover, strategic critical thinking skills are required at every step of research writing. Here you sense the active, questioning, reflective activity of the mind as it confronts a problem, burrows into it, and moves through the problem to a solution, proof, or conclusion. Developing the ability to do research writing thus represents an integration of problem solving and composing talents.

Research writing should be treated as a skill to be developed rather than a trial to be borne. Unfortunately, there are many misconceptions about it. Contrary to conventional wisdom, research does not begin boringly with the library catalog and end with the final period that you add to a bibliographic entry. (In fact, electronic searches and word processing have taken much of the drudgery out of writing research papers.) Nor does research writing exclusively report information, even though some writers tackle a research paper as a bland and boring recitation of facts.

Research actually means the careful investigation of a subject in order to discover or revise facts, theories, or applications. Your purpose is to demonstrate how other researchers approach a problem and how you treat that problem. A good research paper subtly blends your ideas and the attitudes or findings of others. In research writing you are dealing with ideas that are already in the public domain, but you are also contributing to knowledge.

RESEARCH WRITING:
PRECONCEPTIONS AND PRACTICE

When your ideas—rather than the ideas of others—become the center of the research process, writing a research paper becomes dynamic instead of static. The standard preconception about preparing a research paper is that a researcher simply finds a subject and then assembles information from sources usually found in a library. This strategy does teach disciplined habits of work and thought, and it is a traditional way to conduct research for college courses. Yet, does this conventional preconception match the practices of professional researchers?

Consider the following tasks:

- Evaluate critical responses to a best-selling novel, a book of poetry, a CD, or an award-winning film.
- Analyze the impact of the South, the West, or another region on a writer's literary career.
- Investigate a literary scandal of the last century.
- Assess recent responses to Conrad's *Heart of Darkness.*
- Discuss the consequences of recent immigration on literature and film.
- Define feminist fiction, using three writers as the basis for your research.

How would a professional researcher view these projects? First the researcher sees a subject as a *problem,* rather than a mere topic. Often this problem is authorized or designated by a collaborator, an editor, or a person in authority. The researcher has the task of developing or testing a hypothesis stemming from the particular problem: for example, whether or not critics think that Aristotle's theory of drama applies to today's theater. *Hypothesis formation* is at the heart of professional research.

Second, the researcher often has to engage in primary as well as secondary research. *Primary research* relies on your analysis of texts, letters, manuscripts and other materials, whether written, visual, or aural. *Secondary research* relies on sources that comment on the primary sources. For example, a critic's commentary on *Citizen Kane* or a commentary by Irving Howe on William Faulkner's "A Rose for Emily" would be secondary sources; the film itself or Faulkner's story would be primary sources. Because primary are not necessarily more reliable than secondary sources, you must always evaluate the reliability of both types of material. Critics can misinterpret, and experts often disagree, forcing you to weigh evidence and reach your own conclusions.

Third, all researchers face deadlines of a few days, a week, a month, or more. Confronted with deadlines, professional researchers learn to *telescope* their efforts in order to obtain information quickly. Common strategies include telephoning, networking (using personal and professional contacts as well as guides to organizations), browsing or searching on-line, conducting computerized or automated bibliographical searches, and turning to annotated bibliographies (listing articles on the topic with commentaries on each item) and specialized indexes (focusing on a particular field or discipline). Other strategies include turning to review articles, which evaluate other resources, and browsing through current articles, which may provide useful background as well as the most current thinking about the topic. These sources, many of which are found in the reference room of a library, permit the researcher to dive into the middle of a problem, rather than tread water in front of a library catalog.

Finally, much professional researching does not fall neatly into one academic content area. Typically, it cuts across subjects and disciplines, perhaps touching on literature, history, politics, psychology, economics, or more. The interdisciplinary nature of many research projects creates special problems for the researcher, especially in the use of bibliographical materials, which do tend to be subject-oriented. Good researchers know that they cannot be ghetoized into one subject area, such as history of physics. Knowledge in the contemporary era tends increasingly toward interdisciplinary concerns, and you must develop the critical thinking skills needed to operate effectively in an increasingly complex world.

Training, discipline, and strong critical thinking skills are necessary for any form of college research. Such research is not beyond your talents and abilities. Learn how to use library and electronic sources selectively and efficiently, but also learn how to view the world outside your library as a vast laboratory to be used fruitfully in order to solve your research problems.

THE RESEARCH PROCESS

The research process involves thinking, searching, reading, writing, and rewriting. The final product—the research paper—is the result of your discoveries in and contributions to the realm of ideas about your topic. More than any other form of college writing, however, the research paper evolves gradually through a series of stages.

This does not mean you proceed step-by-step through a rigid series of phases. Instead, the act of composing moves back and forth over a series of activities, and the actual act of writing remains unique to the individual researcher. For example, some writers prefer to draft an essay on some problem or issue that they know well and then fill in the research component. This procedure works especially well if you have been assigned a researched essay, requiring a limited number of sources, rather than a full research project. Other researchers are more cautious and conduct research before writing anything. Some writers take notes on note cards; some store information in their computers; others, in the tradition of the journalist, jot down information in looseleaf notebooks. And there are some writers who, with a good internal sense of organization, manage to get by with seemingly chaotic ramblings recorded on any scrap of paper available.

Writers with little experience in developing research papers do have to be more methodical than experienced researchers who streamline and adjust the composing process to the scope and design of their projects. Despite the idiosyncrasies of writers, however, the research process tends to move through several interrelated stages or phases.

PHASES IN THE RESEARCH PROCESS

Phase 1: Defining Your Ojective

Choose a *researchable* topic.

Identify a *problem* inherent in the topic that gives you the reason for writing about the topic.

Examine the *purpose* of or the benefits to be gained from conducting research on the topic.

Think about the assumptions, interests, and needs of your *audience.*

Decide how you are going to *limit* your topic.

Establish a working *hypothesis* to guide and control the scope and direction of your research.

Phase 2: Locating Your Sources

Decide on your *methodology*—the types or varieties of primary and secondary research you plan to conduct. Determine the method of collecting data.

Go to the library and skim a general article or conduct a computer search to *determine if your topic is researchable* and if your hypothesis is likely to stand up.

Develop a *tentative working bibliography,* a file listing sources that seem relevant to your topic.

Review your bibliography and *reassess your topic and hypothesis.*

Phase 3: Gathering and Organizing Data

Obtain your sources, taking notes on all information related directly to your thesis.

Analyze and organize your information. Design a *preliminary outline* with a tentative thesis *if* your findings support your hypothesis.

Revise your thesis if your findings suggest alternative conclusions.

Phase 4: Writing and Submitting the Paper

Write a *rough draft* of the paper, concentrating on the flow of thoughts and integrating research findings into the texture of the report.

Write a *first revision* to tighten organization, improve style, and check on the placement of data. Prepare citations that identify the sources of your information. Assemble a list of the references you have cited in your paper.

Prepare the manuscript using the format called for by the course, the discipline, or the person authorizing the research project.

Phase 1: Defining Your Objective

The first step in research writing is to select a researchable topic. You certainly do not want to discover that your topic for a 1,500-word term paper requires a book to handle it adequately. Nor do you want to risk spending fruitless days investigating a topic that lacks enough available information. Like the bear in the Goldilocks tale, you are in quest of something that is "just right"—a topic that is appropriate in scope for your assignment, a topic that promises an adventure for you in the realm of ideas, and a topic that will interest, if not excite, your audience.

You reduce wasted time and effort if you approach the research project as a problem to be investigated and solved, a controversy to take a position on, or a question to be answered. As a basis, you need a strong hypothesis or working thesis (which may be little more than a hunch or a calculated guess). The point of your investigation is to identify, illustrate, explain, argue, or prove that thesis. Start with a hypothesis before you actually begin to conduct research; otherwise, you will discover that you are simply reading in or about a topic, instead of reading toward the objective of substantiating your thesis or proposition.

Of course, before you can formulate a hypothesis, you need to start with a general idea of what subject you want to explore, what your purpose is going to be, and how you plan to select and limit a topic from your larger subject area. Prewriting strategies can help you find and limit topics for your research project. At the same time, a topic lends itself to research and to hypothesis formation if (1) it strongly interests you, (2) you already know something about it, (3) it raises the sort of questions that require primary and secondary research, and (4) you already have formed some opinions about problems related to it. If you are free to choose a topic in which you are already expert, it will be relatively easy to arrive at a strong, working thesis to serve as the basis for a rewarding research effort. On the other hand, if a professor assigns a topic about which you know little or nothing, you might have to do some background reading before you can develop your hypothesis.

The trick at the outset of the research process is to fit your topic and hypothesis to the demands of the assignment. Your purpose is to solve a *specific* problem, shed light on a *specific* topic, state an opinion on a *specific* controversy, offer *specific* proofs or solutions. Your audience does not want a welter of general information, a bland summary of the known and the obvious, or free associations or meditations on an issue or problem. You know that your audience wants answers; consequently, a way to locate your ideal topic is to ask questions about it.

You may want to ask a series of specific questions about your subject and ultimately combine related questions. Remember to ask your questions in such a way as to pose problems that demand answers. Then try to determine which topic best fits the demands of the assignment and lends itself to the most fruitful and economical method of research.

Phase 2: Locating Your Sources

You have only a certain amount of time in which to locate information for any research project. If you have a sufficiently narrowed topic and a working hypothesis, you at least know what type of information will be most useful for your report. Not all information on a topic is relevant, of course; with a hypothesis you can distinguish between useful and irrelevant material.

To use your time efficiently, you have to *streamline* your method for collecting data. Most research writing for college courses relies heavily on secondary research material available in libraries or on-line. To develop a preliminary list of sources, you should go directly to general reference works if you have to do background reading. If you are already knowledgeable about the subject, begin with resources that permit you to find a continuing series of articles and books on a single issue. Again, you should be moving as rapidly as possible from the general to the specific.

Using the Library Catalog   The library on-line or card catalog lists information by author, title, and subject. Of the three, the subject listings are the best place to look for sources, but they are not necessarily the place to start your research. Begin by determining what your library offers. For instance the on-line catalog may include all library materials or only holdings acquired fairly recently. The catalog also may or may not supply up-to-date information because books may take several years to appear in print and some weeks to be cataloged. Thus you may need to turn to separate indexes of articles, primary documents, and on-line materials for the most current material.

On the other hand, if your library has a consolidated on-line system, you may have immediate access to materials available regionally and to extensive on-line databases. You may be able to use the same terminal to search for books shelved in your own library, materials available locally through the city or county library, and current periodicals listed in specialized databases. Such access can simplify and consolidate your search.

AURARIA LIBRARY

GENDER is in 1561 titles.
ADVERTISING is in 1270 titles.
Both "ADVERTISING" and "GENDER" are in 13 titles.
There are 13 entries with ADVERTISING & GENDER.

| NEXT PAGE | EXTENDED DISPLAY | START OVER | ANOTHER SEARCH | LIMIT THIS SEARCH | (CU-Law) (CSU) (UNC) (DU) |

(DU-Law) (Jeffco)

You searched: WORD ⬍ [gender advertising] (Search)

Num	Mark	WORDS (1-12 of 13)	Entries 13 Found
1	☐	Advertising and culture : theoretical perspectives / edited	1
2	☐	Creating Rosie the Riveter : class, gender, and propaganda d	1
3	☐	Education, technology, power : educational computing as a so	1
4	☐	The Electronic grapevine : rumor, reputation, and reporting	1
5	☐	Feminist perspectives on eating disorders / edited by Patric	1
6	☐	Gender advertisements / Erving Goffman.	1
7	☐	Global and multinational advertising / edited by Basil G. En	1
8	☐	Inarticulate longings : The ladies' home journal, gender, an	1
9	☐	Putting on appearances : gender and advertising / Diane Bart	1
10	☐	Russian cultural studies : an introduction / edited by Catri	1
11	☐	Sport business : operational and theoretical aspects / [edit	1
12	☐	Undressing the ad : reading culture in advertising / edited	1

(Save Marked Records) (JUMP TO) [13]

| NEXT PAGE | EXTENDED DISPLAY | START OVER | ANOTHER SEARCH | LIMIT THIS SEARCH | (CU-Law) (CSU) (UNC) (DU) (DU-Law) |

(Jeffco)

Search Other Regional Libraries:

 Denver Public Library   Colorado State Publications

Subject indexing can be useful when you are researching a topic around which a considerable body of information and analysis has already developed. Identify as many key words (terms that identify and describe your subject) or relevant subject classifications as possible. Use these same terms as you continue your search for sources, and add additional terms identified in the entries you find. The example on this page illustrates a key word search for materials on gender issues and advertising.

Clicking on the Extended Display option for an item supplies full bibliographic information as well as the location of the book in the library and its availability. Information for the fourth item listed above appears on the next page.

Checking General Reference Sources General reference sources include encyclopedias, dictionaries, handbooks, atlases, biographies, almanacs, yearbooks, abstracts, and annual reviews of scholarship within a field. Many of

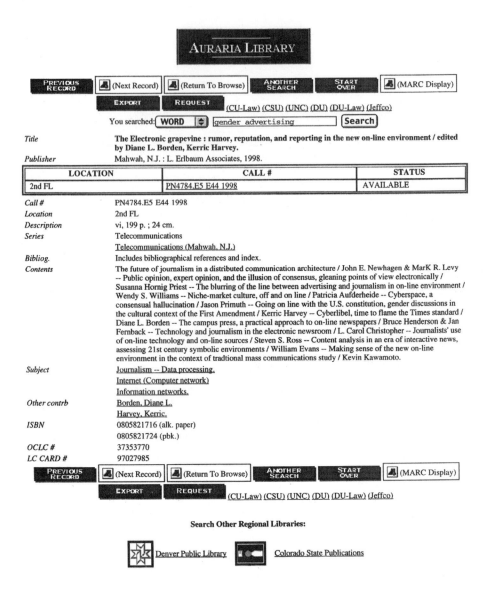

these sources are available both in print and in an electronic format, on CD-ROM or on-line. Begin your search for these sources in your library's reference room. General reference sources can be useful for background reading and for an introduction to your topic. The bibliographies they contain (such as those that end articles in an encyclopedia) are generally limited, however, and frequently out-of-date. If you want to be a professional researcher, you should not rely exclusively on general reference sources to solve your research problems.

Searching Indexes and Databases   Electronic and print indexes and databases can efficiently lead you to up-to-date articles in journals, magazines, and newspapers. Indexes usually list materials that you will then need to locate. Some databases, however, may include complete texts of articles or even books. Ask a reference librarian about the terminals available in your library for accessing materials on CD-ROM or on-line. If you need historical information or want to trace a topic backwards in time, however, you may need to use print indexes as well because electronic sources may date back only a few years or cover only a certain number of years.

The following indexes and databases are just a few of the many resources that are widely available. Some are general; others are specialized by discipline or field. Such indexes supply ready access to a wide array of useful materials, including articles, books, newspaper stories, statistics, and government documents. Ask the librarian in the reference area or the catalog area whether these are available in print or on-line.

General Resources

American Statistics Index

Congressional Information Service Index

Expanded Academic Index

FirstSearch Catalog

Magazine Index

National Newspaper Index

New York Times Index

SocSci Search

UnCover

Specialized Resources

America: History and Life

Arts and Humanities Search

Book Review Digest

Electric Library

Essay and General Literature Index

Expanded Academic Index

ERIC (Educational Resources Information Center)

Film Literature Index

Gale Literary Index

Granger's

Humanities Index

Index to Book Reviews in the Humanities Literature Resource Center

Magillon Authors

Magillon Literature

MLA (Modern Language Association) International Bibliography

PsychLit

Social Sciences Index

Wilsondisc: Humanities Index

Women's Studies Index

Each index or database restricts the sources it lists in specific ways, based on the particular topics covered or the types of sources included. For example, the full title of the *MLA Bibliography* indicates that it lists "Books and Articles on the Modern Languages and Literatures." Besides books and articles, however, it includes essays or chapters collected in a book, conference papers, films, recordings, and other similar sources, but it does not list summaries or encyclopedia articles. Its primary subjects include literary criticism, literary themes and genres, linguistics, and folklore. Thus, you can search for an author's name, a title, a literary period, or subjects as varied as hoaxes, metaphysical poetry, and self-knowledge, all in relationship to studies in language and literature. This bibliography is available in print, on CD-ROM, on-line, or in other electronic versions. The print version is published every year, but the on-line version is updated 10 times during the year. A search of the *MLA Bibliography 1/81–11/97* on CD-ROM for information on gender issues in advertising would turn up items such as the following:

TI: The Coining of a Separate Women's Language: American <u>Advertising</u> for Women in the 1920s
AU: Brogger, -Fredrik-Chr.
SO: Nordlyd: -Tromso-University-Working-Papers-in-Language-and-Linguistics, Tromso, Norway (Nordlyd). 1995, 23, 271–85
AN: 96094934

TI: Fashion in the Age of <u>Advertising</u>
AU: Martin, -Richard
SO: Journal-of-Popular-Culture, Bowling Green, OH (JPC). 1995
Fall, 29:2, 235-54
AN: 96028795

As your search progresses and your hypothesis evolves, you will find resources even more specifically focused on your interests.

Finding On-line Materials   Your library, your college Web site, or your instructor's home page may list useful sites on the World Wide Web, organized by discipline or interest area. On-line clearinghouses and print materials about the Web also identify especially useful sites for researchers. Once you have located an Internet address—a URL (universal resource locator)—for a site on the World Wide Web, you can go directly to that location. The end of the address can help you assess the kind of location you will reach.

.org = nonprofit organizations, including professional groups

.edu = colleges, universities, and other educational institutions

.com= businesses and commercial enterprises

.gov = government branches and agencies

.mil = branches of the military

.net = major computer networks

If you need to search the Internet for sources, try using one of the search engines supplied by your Internet access program. Search engines such as Alta Vista, Google, Excite, Infoseek, Lycos, HotBot, or Yahoo! hunt through vast numbers of pages at Web sites, seeking those that mention key words that you specify. The search engine then supplies you with a list, usually ten items at a time, of those sites. Given the enormous number of Web sites and their component pages, you need to select your search items carefully so that you locate reasonable numbers of pertinent sources.

A Web page may supply links to other useful sites. If you click on the link, usually highlighted or in color, you can go directly to that related site. For example, the site on the next page *(http://www.fedworld.gov/),* sponsored by the federal government, includes links to federal databases and two forms of key word searches that can lead to particular resources.

Following a chain of links requires critical thinking to assess whether each link seems reliable and current. This kind of research also can take a great deal of time, especially if you explore each link and then follow it to the next. As you move from link to link, keep your hypothesis in mind so that you are not distracted from your central purpose.

In order to gain expert information, you may wish to contact an informed individual directly by e-mail, following up on contact information supplied at a Web site or through other references. If your topic is of long-term interest to you and you have plenty of time to do your research, you may want to join a *listserv* or *e-mail conference,* a group of people interested in a particular topic, whose messages are sent automatically to all participants. Exchanges among those interested in a topic may also be posted on a *bulletin board server* or a *newsgroup,* where you can read both past and ongoing messages and exchanges. The information you receive from others may be very authoritative

FedWorld.gov

A program of the United States Department of Commerce

About   Search   Contact   Databases

Site Revised 1999 May 18
File, Jobs and Web Databases Updated Daily

Browse the FedWorld Information Network
Pick From List:

| List FedWorld Databases | ⬍ | Go! |

Search Web Pages on the FedWorld Information Network
Enter some keywords:

| | Search |

Search for U.S. Government Reports
Enter some keywords:

| | Search |

Explore U.S. Government Web Sites

About FedWorld   About NTIS   FedWorld Services For U.S. Government Agencies

Points of Contact at FedWorld   Privacy   Security

National Technical Information Service
Technology Administration
U.S. Department of Commerce
Springfield, VA 22161
703-605-6000
Send comments to webmaster@fedworld.gov

Hammer Award Winner

and reliable, but it may also represent the biased viewpoint of the individual. Assess it carefully by comparing it with information from other sources—print as well as electronic.

Using Nonprint Sources In the library and on-line, you have access to potentially useful nonprint materials of all kinds—videos, CD-ROMs, films, slides, works of art, records of performances, or other sources that might relate to your topic. When you search for these sources, you may find them in your library's main catalog or in a separate listing. In the catalog entry, be sure to note the location of the source and its access hours, especially if they are limited. If you need a projector or other equipment to use the material, ask the reference librarian where you go to find such equipment.

Developing Field Resources   You may want to *interview* an expert, *survey* the opinions of other students, *observe* an event or situation, or examine it over a long period of time as a *case study.* Ask your instructor's advice as you design questions for an interview or a survey or procedures for a short- or long-term observation. Also be sure to find out whether you need permission to conduct this kind of research on campus or in the community.

The questions you ask will determine the nature and extent of the responses that you receive; as a result, your questions should be developed after you have established clear objectives for your field research. You also need to plan how you will analyze the answers before, not after, you administer the questionnaire or conduct the interview. Once you have drafted interview or survey questions, test them by asking your friends or classmates to respond. Use these preliminary results to revise any ambiguous questions and to test your method of analysis. If you are an observer, establish in advance what you will observe, how you will record your observations, and how you will analyze them. Get permission, if needed, from the site where you will conduct your observation. Your field sources can help you expand your knowledge of the topic, see its applications or discover real-world surprises, or locate more sources, whether print, electronic, or field.

Preparing a Working Bibliography   The purpose of compiling a working bibliography is to keep track of possible sources, to determine the nature and extent of the information available, to provide a complete and accurate list of sources to be presented in the paper, and to make preparing the final bibliography much easier. Include in your working bibliography all sources that you have a hunch are potentially useful. After all, you may not be able to obtain all the items listed, and some material will turn out to be useless, repetitious, or irrelevant to your topic. Such entries can easily be eliminated at a later stage when you prepare your final bibliography.

One way to simplify the task of preparing your final Works Cited or References section is to use a standard form for your working bibliography, whether you use cards or computer entries. The models given later in this chapter are based on two guides, abbreviated as MLA and APA. The *MLA Handbook for Writers of Research Papers* (New York: Modern Language Association of America, 1999; 5th ed.) is generally followed in English, foreign languages, and other fields in the humanities. Instructors in the social sciences, natural sciences, education, and business are likely to favor the style presented in the *Publication Manual of the American Psychological Association* (Washington, DC: American Psychological Association, 2001; 5th ed.). Because the preferred form of citation of sources varies considerably from field to field, check with your instructors to determine which of these two formats they prefer or if they recommend another style. Follow any specific directions from an instructor carefully.

INFORMATION FOR A WORKING BIBLIOGRAPHY

Record the following information for a book:

1. Name(s) of author(s)
2. Title of book, underlined
3. Place of publication
4. Publisher's name
5. Date of publication
6. Call number or location in library
7. URL and date of access on-line

Record the following information for an article in a periodical:

1. Name(s) of author(s)
2. Title of article, in quotation marks
3. Title of periodical, underlined
4. Volume number or issue number
5. Date of publication
6. Page numbers on which article appears
7. Call number or location in library
8. URL and date of access on-line

As you search for relevant articles and books, you should take down complete information on each item on a 3 × 5 note card or start a bibliographic file on your computer. Complete information, properly recorded, will save you the trouble of having to scurry back to the library or back to a Web page for missing data when typing your final bibliography. Be sure to list the item's call number and location in the library or its URL; then you can easily find the material once you are ready to begin reading and relocate it if you need to refer to it again. When preparing bibliography cards for entries listed in annotated bibliographies, citation indexes, and abstracts, you might want to jot down notes from any pertinent summaries that are provided. Complete a separate card or file entry for each item that you think is promising.

Author	Dávidházi, Péter
Title	The Romantic Cult of Shakespeare: Literary Reception in Anthropological Perspective
Place of publication	New York
	St. Martin's Press
Date of publication	1998
Location	Call Number: PR 2979.H8.D38.1998

If you use your computer to record bibliographic information, you may want to find software designed for this purpose. Your software may provide database categories or options from which you can select the categories required by the style guide you need to use. You also can use the requirements of your style guide to help you develop your own, such as these for a book.

Author's last name:	Pinker
Author's first name:	Steven
Book title:	**The Language Instinct: How the Mind Creates Language**
Publisher's location:	**New York**
Publisher (imprint):	**HarperCollins Publishers (HarperPerennial)**
Date published (original date):	**1995 (1994)**

Once you begin to build a bibliographic database, you can refer to your listings and supplement them each time you are assigned a paper.

Reassessing Your Topic   Once you have compiled your working bibliography, take the time to reassess the entire project before you get more deeply involved in it. Analyze your bibliography cards carefully to determine whether you should proceed to the next stage of information gathering.

Your working bibliography should send out signals that help you shape your thinking about the topic. The dominant signal should indicate that your topic is not too narrow or too broad. Generally, a bibliography of ten to fifteen promising entries for a 1,500-word paper indicates that your topic might be properly limited at this stage. A listing of only three or four entries signals that you must expand the topic or consider discarding it. Conversely, a listing of a hundred entries warns that you might be working yourself into a research swamp.

Another signal from your working bibliography should help you decide whether your hypothesis is on target or could be easily recast to make it more precise. Entry titles, abstracts, and commentaries on articles are excellent sources of confirmation. If established scholarship does not support your hypothesis, it would be best to discard your hypothesis and begin again.

Finally, the working bibliography should provide signals about the categories or parts of your research. Again, titles, abstracts, and commentaries are useful. In other words, as you compile the entries, you can begin to think through the problem and to perceive contours of thought that will dictate the organization of the paper even before you begin to do detailed research. Your working bibliography should be alive with such signals.

Phase 3: Gathering and Organizing Data

If your working bibliography confirms the value, logic, and practicality of your research project, you can then move to the next phase of the research process: taking notes and organizing information. Information shapes and refines your thinking; you move from an overview to a more precise understanding, analysis, and interpretation of the topic. By the end of this third phase, you should be able to transform your hypothesis into a thesis and your assembled notes into an outline.

Evaluating Sources   Your preliminary task as you move into the third phase is to immerse yourself in articles, books, and perhaps primary research sources, but not to drown in them. Begin by skimming your sources. Skimming is not random reading or casual perusal, but a careful examination of the material to sort out the valuable sources from the not-so-valuable ones. For a book, check the table of contents and index for information on your topic; then determine whether the information is relevant to your problem. For an article, see if the abstract or topic sentences in the body of the essay confirm your research interests.

CRITERIA FOR ASSESSING THE VALUE OF A SOURCE FOR YOUR PROJECT

1. Is the source directly relevant to your topic?
2. Does it discuss the topic extensively?
3. Does it bear on your hypothesis, supporting, qualifying, or contradicting it?
4. Does it present relatively current information, especially for research in the social and natural sciences?

Besides being pertinent to your research problem, a source needs to be reliable. Books and articles in print have generally been reviewed by editors and experts in the field, but materials located on the World Wide Web or elsewhere on the Internet may or may not have been examined by unbiased or authoritative experts.

CRITERIA FOR EVALUATING SOURCES FOR YOUR PROJECT

Evaluating Print Sources

1. Is the author a credible authority? Does the book jacket, preface, or byline indicate the author's background, education, or other publications? Do other writers refer to this source and accept it as reliable? Is the publisher or publication reputable?

2. Does the source provide information comparable to that in other reputable sources?
3. Does the source seem accurate and authoritative, or does it make claims that are not generally accepted?
4. Does the source seem unbiased, or does it seem to promote a particular business, industry, organization, political position, or philosophy?
5. Does the source supply notes, a bibliography, or other information to document its sources?
6. If the source has been published recently, does it include current information? Are its sources current or dated?
7. Does the source seem carefully edited and printed?

Evaluating Web Sites or Other Electronic Sources

1. Is the author identified? Is the site sponsored by a reputable business, agency, or organization? Does the site supply information so that you can contact the author or the sponsor?
2. Does the site provide information comparable to that in other reputable sources, including print sources?
3. Does the site seem accurate and authoritative or quirky and idiosyncratic?
4. Does the site seem unbiased, or is it designed to promote a particular business, industry, organization, political position, or philosophy?
5. Does the site supply appropriate, useful links? Do these links seem current and relevant? Do most of them work? Does the site document sources for the information it supplies directly?
6. Has the site been updated or revised recently?
7. Does the site seem carefully designed? Is it easy and logical to navigate? Are its graphics well integrated and related to the site's overall purpose or topic? Is the text carefully edited?

Taking Notes   Once you have a core of valuable material, you can begin to read these sources closely and take detailed notes. Skillful note taking requires a subtle blend of critical thinking skills. It is not a matter of recording all the information available or simply copying long quotes. You want to select and summarize the general ideas that will form the outline of your paper, to record specific evidence to support your ideas, and to copy exact statements you plan to quote for evidence or interest. You also want to add your own ideas and evaluation of the material. All the notes you take must serve the specific purpose of your paper as it is stated in your hypothesis. Paraphrase, summary, and quotation are crucial notetaking skills.

Alternatives for taking notes include using 5 × 8 note cards, setting up a computer file for your notes, writing on one side of separate pages in a notebook, or combining these systems with on-line and library printouts. In any case, take brief and precise notes. Look for the crisp quotation, the telling statistic, the insight by a leading authority, the sound original idea. Always keep your hypothesis in mind to limit your note taking.

GUIDELINES FOR TAKING NOTES ABOUT YOUR TOPIC

1. Write the author's last name, the title of the source, and the page number at the top of each card or entry. (Complete information on the source should already have been recorded on a bibliography card or listed in an entry in a computer file.)
2. Record only one idea or a group of closely related facts on each card or in each entry.
3. List a subtopic at the top of the card or entry. This will permit you to arrange your cards or entries from various sources into groups, and these groups can then serve as the basis of your outline.
4. List three types of information: (a) summaries of material; (b) paraphrases of material, in which you recast the exact words of the author; and (c) direct quotations, accurately transcribed.
5. Add your own ideas at the bottom of the card or following specific notes.

The sample note cards printed below illustrate useful arrangements of research information.

Topic label	*cult-definition*
Author of book or article	*Dávidházi*
Relevant page numbers	*pp. 8–21*
Direct quotation	*8: Defines "cult and culture in terms of their specific attitudes, their different ritual and their respective ways of using language."*
Student's commentary	*Is this a matter of degree? (How do you tell the difference?)*

Topic label	*cult-definition*
Author of book or article	*Dávidházi*
Relevant page numbers	*pp. 8–21*
Paraphrase	*8: The first criteria for a literary cult is an attitude that is worshipful, a feeling like religious reverence. The next lies in behavior that celebrates the literary figure, including both verbalizing praise and attending ritual events, such as festivals and trips to Stratford. Finally, the glorified language used to describe the figure is extreme.*
Student's commentary	*(useful list—does it relate to the Shakespeare festival on campus during the summer?)*

The following example illustrates how you might enter notes in a computer file. The nature and scope of your paper may help you figure out how to organize your files. For example, you could set up a separate file for each source or for each main topic. Each note might start at the top of a new page. Once your notes are entered, you can easily copy quotations from your note file to your paper or use your computer's search system to hunt for a key word.

Topic:	language community
Source:	Pinker
Page numbers:	pp. 15–16
Quotation/ Summary/ Paraphrase:	Q. 16: "In any natural history of the human species, language would stand out as the pre-eminent trait. [. . .] A common language connects the members of a community into an information-sharing network with formidable collective powers."
Comment:	I like the book's example of the Tower of Babel as a key story. It shows what happens if people work on communicating with each other.

When you have completed all your research, organize your notes under the various subtopics or subheadings that you have established. If possible or desirable, try to combine some subtopics and eliminate others so that you have between three and five major categories for analysis and development. You are now ready to develop an outline for the research essay.

Designing an Outline   Because you must organize a lot of material in a clear way, an outline is especially valuable in a research essay. Some experts actually recommend that you develop an outline before you conduct research, but this is possible only if your bibliographical search and your own general knowledge of the topic permit establishing subtopics at that early stage.

Most importantly, now is the time to establish your thesis. By reviewing your notes and assessing the data, you should be able to transform the calculated guess that was your hypothesis into a much firmer thesis. Focus your attention on your thesis by stating it at the top of the page where you are working on your outline.

Spend as much time as is reasonable drafting an outline. For a rough outline, you can simply list your general subheadings and their supporting data. However, the recommended strategy is to work more systematically through your notes and compile as full an outline as possible, one that develops each point logically and in detail. If you are required to submit an outline with your research paper, you should begin to develop a full, formal outline at this stage. Such an outline would look like this:

I.
   A.
   B.
      1.
      2.
      3.
         a.
         b.
II.

Use roman numerals for your most important points, capital letters for the next most important points, arabic numbers for supporting points, and lower-case letters for pertinent details or minor points.

Phase 4: Writing and Submitting the Paper

As you enter the fourth and final phase of the research process, keep in mind that a research paper is a formal essay, not a jagged compilation of notes. You should be prepared to take your research effort through several increasingly polished versions, most likely at least a rough draft, a revised draft, and a final manuscript.

Writing the Rough Draft   For your rough draft, concentrate on filling in the shape of your outline. If your notes are out of sequence or scattered to the four corners of your room, take the time to rearrange them in the topic order that your outline assumes. In this way you will be able to integrate notes and writing more efficiently and effectively.

Even as you adhere to your formal outline in beginning the rough draft you should also be open to better possibilities and prospects for presenting ideas and information. Often you discover that an outline is too rigid, that a minor idea needs greater emphasis, that something important has been left out entirely, even that your thesis needs further adjustment. There are potentially dozens of shifts, modifications, and improvements that you can make as you transfer the form of an outline to an actual written paper. Although your primary effort in writing a first draft is to rough out the shape and content of your paper, the flow of your ideas will often be accompanied by self-adjusting operations of your mind, all aimed at making your research effort even better than you thought it could be at the outline stage.

Whether or not you incorporate quotations from your notes into the rough draft is a matter of preference. Some writers prefer to transcribe quotations and paraphrases at this point in order to save time at a later stage. Other writers copy and insert these materials directly from entries in a computer file for notes. Still others feel their thought processes are interrupted by having to write out quoted and paraphrased material and to design transitions between their own writing and the transcribed material. They simply write "insert" in the draft with a reference to the appropriate notes.

The need to integrate material from several sources tests your reasoning ability during the writing of the rough draft. For any given subtopic in your outline, you will be drawing together information from a variety of sources. To an extent, your outline will tell you how to arrange some of this information. At the same time, you must contribute your own commentary, arrange details in an effective order, and sort out conflicting claims and interpretations. A great deal of thinking as well as writing goes into the design of your first draft.

It is critical thinking and problem solving as much as the act of writing that makes for a successful rough draft. As you draft, you are actually solving a complex research problem in your own words. For the moment, you do not have to worry about the polished state of your words. You do, however, have to be certain that the intelligence that you are bringing to bear on the design of your paper is adequate to the challenge. You are not involved in a dull transcription of material when writing the rough draft of a research paper. Instead, you are engaged in a demanding effort to think your way through a problem of considerable magnitude, working in a logical way from the introduction and the statement of your thesis, through the evidence, to the outcome or conclusion that supports everything that has come before.

Revising the Draft   If you can put your rough draft away for a day or two, you can return to it with the sharpened and objective eye of a critical reviewer. In the rough draft you thought and wrote your way through the problem. Now you must rethink and rewrite in order to give better form and expression to your ideas.

Use the guidelines outlined below to approach your revision. Consider every aspect of your paper, from the most general to the most specific. Look again at the organization of the whole paper, key topics, paragraphs, and sentences; read through for clarity of expression and details of grammar, punctuation, and spelling. A comprehensive revision effort will result in a decidedly more polished version of your paper.

GUIDELINES FOR REVISING
YOUR RESEARCH WRITING

1. Does my title illuminate the topic of the essay and capture the reader's interest?
2. Have I created the proper tone to meet the expectations of my audience?
3. Does my opening paragraph hook the reader? Does it clearly establish and limit the topic? Is my thesis statement clear, limited, and interesting?
4. Do all my body paragraphs support the thesis? Is there a single topic and main idea for each paragraph? Do I achieve unity, coherence, and proper development? Is there sufficient evidence in each paragraph to support the main idea?

(continued)
   5. Are there clear and effective transitions linking my ideas within and between paragraphs?
   6. Have I selected the best strategies to meet the demands of the assignment and the expectations of my audience?
   7. Are all my assertions clearly stated, defined, and supported? Do I use sound logic and avoid faulty reasoning? Do I acknowledge other people's ideas properly?
   8. Is my conclusion strong and effective?
   9. Are my sentences grammatically correct? Have I avoided errors in the use of verbs, pronouns, adjectives, and prepositions? Have I corrected errors of agreement?
  10. Are my sentences complete? Have I corrected all fragments, comma splices, and fused sentences?
  11. Have I varied my sentences effectively? Have I employed clear coordination and subordination? Have I avoided awkward constructions?
  12. Is my use of periods, commas, semicolons, and other forms of punctuation correct?
  13. Are all words spelled correctly? Do my words mean what I think they mean? Are they specific? Are they concrete? Is my diction appropriate to college writing? Is my language free of clichés slang, jargon, and euphemism? Do I avoid needless abstractions? Is my usage sound?
  14. Have I carefully attended to such mechanical matters as apostrophes, capitals, numbers, and word divisions?
  15. Does my manuscript conform to acceptable guidelines for submitting typewritten work?

Preparing the Final Manuscript   Leave time in your research effort to prepare a neat, clean, attractively designed manuscript using a typewriter or computer. Store your word processor file on a backup disk, and print or duplicate an extra copy of the report. Submit a neat, clear version, and keep the second copy. Consult your instructor for the desired format, and carefully follow the guidelines for manuscript preparation in your final version. Look also at the sample paper at the end of this chapter, which illustrates how to present the final version of a paper in accordance with MLA style (see pages 148–158). Having invested so much time and effort in a research project, you owe it to yourself as well as to the reader to submit a manuscript that has been prepared with extreme care.

DOCUMENTING SOURCES

Documentation is an essential part of any research paper. Documenting your sources throughout the paper and in a section called Works Cited or References tells your audience just how well you have conducted your research. It offers readers the opportunity to check on authorities, to do further reading, and to assess the originality of your contribution to an established body of opinion. Neglect of proper documentation can destroy your research effort. It can also be *plagiarism*—the use of material without giving credit to the source, or, put more seriously, the theft of material that properly belongs to other thinkers, writers, and researchers.

Quotations, paraphrases, and summaries obviously require credit, for they are the actual words or the theories or interpretations of others. Paraphrases and summaries also frequently offer statistics or data that are not well known, and this type of information also requires documentation. Facts in a controversy (facts open to dispute or to varying interpretations) also fall within the realm of documentation.

Besides giving appropriate credit to others for their words and ideas, be careful either to quote exactly or to paraphrase or summarize using your own words and your own sentence structures. For example, avoid a paraphrase that simply replaces a few key words in a sentence. Like wording copied directly without giving credit to its source, such a paraphrase may be considered plagiarism. Even if you do credit your source, such a close paraphrase makes your research seem sloppy and poorly conducted. Aim instead at recasting the writer's ideas in your own words.

MATERIALS THAT REQUIRE DOCUMENTATION

1. Direct quotations
2. Paraphrased material
3. Summarized material
4. Any key idea or opinion adapted and incorporated into your paper
5. Specific data (whether quoted, paraphrased, or tabulated)
6. Disputed facts

Parenthetical documentation—briefly identifying sources within parentheses in the text—is the most common method of indicating sources. The purpose of a parenthetical citation is to identify a source briefly yet clearly enough that it can be located in the list of references at the end of the paper. In MLA style, the author's last name and the page number in the source are included. APA style uses the author's last name and the year of publication; page numbers are included primarily for direct quotations. Then complete information is listed, alphabetically by author or title (if a source has no specific author), in the Works Cited or References section following the text of the paper. The bibliographic information you have collected should provide you with the details needed for the preparation of both parenthetical documentation and a list of sources.

GENERAL GUIDELINES
FOR PARENTHETICAL DOCUMENTATION

1. Give enough information so that the reader can readily identify the source in the Works Cited (MLA) or References (APA) section of your paper.
2. Supply the citation information in parentheses placed where the material occurs in your text.
3. Give the specific information required by the documentation system you are using, especially when dealing with multivolume works, editions, newspapers, and legal documents.
4. Make certain that the complete sentence containing the parenthetical documentation is readable and grammatically correct.

With your parenthetical documentation prepared, turn your attention next to a final Works Cited or References section. To prepare this list of sources, you simply have to transcribe those bibliography cards or entries that you actually used to write your paper, following the appropriate format.

GENERAL GUIDELINES FOR PREPARING
A LIST OF SOURCES

1. Use the title *Works Cited* (MLA) or *References* (APA).
2. Include only works actually cited in the research paper unless directed otherwise by your instructor.
3. Arrange all works alphabetically according to author's last name or according to the title of a work if there is no author. Ignore *A, An,* or *The.*
4. Begin each entry at the left margin. Indent everything in an entry that comes after the first line by five spaces or 1/2 inch (MLA style) or by five to seven spaces (following APA style for students, unless your instructor directs otherwise).
5. Double-space every line.
6. Punctuate with periods after the three main divisions in most entries—author, title, and publishing information.

In the following sections, you will find examples of MLA and APA documentation forms. Use these examples to help you cite your sources efficiently and clearly.

MLA (Modern Language Association) Documentation   133

MLA (MODERN LANGUAGE ASSOCIATION) DOCUMENTATION

The following examples illustrate how to cite a source in the text and in the list of works cited at the end of a paper.

MLA Parenthetical Documentation   The simplest MLA entry includes the author's last name and the page number, identifying exactly where the quotation or information is located. If the author's name is included in the text, it does not need to be repeated in the citation.

Page Number(s) for a Book
    The play offers what many audiences have found a satisfying conclusion (Hansberry 265–76).

    Garcia Marquez uses another particularly appealing passage as the opening of the story (105).

Volume and Page Number(s) for One Volume of a Multivolume Work
    A strong interest in this literature in the 1960s and 1970s inevitably led to "a significant reassessment of the aesthetic and humanistic achievements of black writers" (Inge, Duke, and Bryer 1: v).

Page Number(s) for an Article in a Journal or Magazine
    Barlow's description of the family members includes "their most notable strengths and weaknesses" (18).

Section and Page Number(s) for a Newspaper Article
    A report on achievement standards for high school courses found "significant variation among schools" (Mallory B1).

Page Number(s) for a Work without an Author
    Computerworld has developed a thoughtful editorial on the issue of government and technology ("Uneasy Silence" 54).

Page Number(s) for a Work by a Group or an Organization
    The Commission on the Humanities has concluded that "the humanities are inescapably bound to literacy" (69).

Page Number(s) for Several Works by One Author
In <u>The Coming Fury</u>, Catton identifies the "disquieting omens" (6) which precede the Civil War.

As Catton concludes his history of the Civil War, he notes that "it began with one act of madness and it ended with another" (<u>Never Call Retreat</u> 457).

Page Number(s) for One Work Quoted in Another
Samuel Johnson praises <u>She Stoops to Conquer</u> because Goldsmith's play achieves "the great end of comedy—making an audience merry" (qtd. in Boswell 171).

MLA List of Works Cited   Following your paper, list the references you have cited in alphabetical order on a separate page entitled "Works Cited." See the Works Cited page of the sample paper (page 158) for an illustration of how you should prepare this page. Use the following sample entries to help you format your references in MLA style. Pay special attention to abbreviated names of publishers, full names of authors, details of punctuation, and other characteristic features of MLA citations.

Work with One Author
Notice the punctuation and underlining in the basic entry for a book.

Aldrich, Marcia. <u>Girl Rearing</u>. New York: Norton, 1998.

Muller, Eddie. <u>Dark City: The Lost World of Film Noir</u>. New York: St. Martin's-Griffin, 1998.

Several Works by One Author
If you use several books or articles by one author, list the author's name in the initial entry. In the next entry or entries, replace the name with the three hypens.

Aldrich, John Herbert. <u>Why Parties? The Origin and Transformation of Political Parties in America</u>. Chicago: U of Chicago P, 1995.

———. <u>Before the Convention: Strategies and Choices in Presidential Nomination Campaigns</u>. Chicago: U of Chicago P, 1980.

Work with Two or Three Authors or Editors
List the names of several authors in the sequence in which they appear in the book or article. Begin with the last name of the author listed first because it is used to determine the alphabetical order for entries. Then identify the other authors by first and last names.

Oakes, Jill, and Rick Riewe. <u>Spirit of Siberia: Traditional Native Life, Clothing, and Footwear</u>. Washington, DC: Smithsonian Inst. P, 1998.

Trueba, Henry T., Grace Pung Guthrie, and Kathryn Hu-Pei Au, eds. <u>Culture and the Bilingual Classroom: Studies in Classroom Ethnography</u>. Rowley: Newbury, 1981.

Work with More than Three Authors or Editors
Name all those involved, or list only the first author or editor with *et al.,* for
"and others."

> Nordhus, Inger, Gary R. VandenBos, Stig Berg, and Pia Fromholt, eds.
> Clinical Geropsychology. Washington, DC: APA, 1998.

> Nordhus, Inger, et al., eds. Clinical Geropsychology. Washington, DC: APA, 1998.

Work with Group or an Organization as Author
> National PTA. National Standards for Parent/Family Involvement Pro-
> grams. Chicago: National PTA, 1997.

Work without An Author
> A Visual Dictionary of Art. Greenwich, CT: New York Graphic Society, 1974.

Work in a Collection of Pieces All by the Same Author
> Malamud, Bernard. "The Assistant." A Malamud Reader. New York: Far-
> rar, 1967. 750–95.

Work in a Collection of Pieces by Different Authors
> McCorkle, Jill. "Final Vinyl Days." It's Only Rock and Roll: An Anthology
> of Rock and Roll Short Stories. Ed. Janice Eidus and John Kastan.
> Boston: Godine, 1998. 19–33.

Collection of Pieces Cited as a Whole
> Weston-Lews, Aidan, ed. Effigies and Ecstasies: Roman Baroque Sculpture and
> Design in the Age of Bernini. Edinburgh: Natl. Gallery of Scotland, 1998.

Work in Several Volumes
> Walther, Ingo F. Art of the 20th Century. 2 vols. Cologne: Taschen, 1998.

Work Translated from Another Language
The first entry below emphasizes the work of the original author by placing
his name first. The next example shifts emphasis to the work of the translators
by identifying them first.

> Rostand, Edmund. Cyrano de Bergerac. Trans. Anthony Burgess. New
> York: Applause, 1998.

> Young, David, and Jiann I. Lin, trans. The Clouds Float North: The Complete
> Poems of Du Xuanji. Bilingual Edition. Hanover: Wesleyan UP, 1998.

Work Appearing as Part of a Series
> Rohn, Suzanne. The Wizard of Oz: Shaping an Imaginary World.
> Twayne's Masterwork Studies 167. New York: Twayne-Simon, 1998.

New Edition of an Older Book
> Wharton, Edith. The Custom of the Country. 1913. NY Public Library Col-
> lector's Edition. New York: Doubleday, 1998.

Entry from a Reference Volume
Treat less common reference books like other books, including place of publication, publisher, and date. For encyclopedias, dictionaries, and other familiar references, simply note the edition and its date. No page numbers are needed if the entries appear in alphabetical order in the reference volume.

"Fox, Luke." Encyclopedia Americana: International Edition. 1996 ed.

Minton, John. "Worksong." American Folklore: An Encyclopedia. Ed. Jan Harold Brunvold. New York: Garland, 1996.

Work Issued by a Federal, State, or Other Government Agency
Depending on the emphasis you intend, you can start with either the writer or the government agency responsible for the publication. "GPO" stands for "Government Printing Office," the publisher of most federal documents.

Brock, Dan W. "An Assessment of the Ethical Issues Pro and Con." Cloning Human Beings. National Bioethics Advisory Commission. Vol. 2. Rockville, MD: GPO, 1997. E1-E23.

National Bioethics Advisory Commission. Cloning Human Beings. 2 vols. Rockville, MD: GPO, 1997.

United States. Cong. House. Subcommittee on Oversight and Investigations of the Committee on Education and the Workforce. Education at a Crossroads: What Works and What's Wasted in Education Today. 105th Cong., 2nd sess. Washington, DC: GPO, 1998.

US Const. Art. 9.

Reference to a Legal Document
When you discuss court cases in your paper, underline their names. In your Works Cited, do not underline them.

Aguilar v. Felton. 473 US 402. 1985.

Article in a Journal with Pagination Continuing through Each Volume
Pistol, Todd A. "Unfinished Business: Letters from a Father to His Son, 1922–1928." Journal of Men's Studies 7 (1999): 215–31.

Article in a Journal with Pagination Continuing Only through Each Issue
Add the issue number after the volume number.

Guyer, Jane I. "Traditions of Invention in Equatorial Africa." African Studies Review 39.3 (1996): 1–28.

Article in a Weekly or Biweekly Periodical
Cowley, Geoffrey. "Cancer and Diet." Newsweek 30 Nov. 1998: 60–66.

Lemonick, Michael D. "The Biological Mother Lode." Time 16 Nov. 1998: 96–97.

Article in a Monthly or Bimonthly Periodical
If an article in a magazine or a newspaper does not continue on consecutive pages, follow the page number on which it begins with a plus sign.

> Blow, Richard. "The Great American Whale Hunt." <u>Mother Jones</u>
> Sept–Oct. 1998: 49+.

Article in a Daily Newspaper
> Morson, Berny. "Tuft-eared Cats Make Tracks in Colorado." <u>Denver</u>
> <u>Rocky Mountain News</u> 4 Feb. 1999: 5A+.

Article with No Author
> "Iguanas Cruise the Caribbean." <u>New Scientist</u> 10 Oct. 1998: 25.

> "People in the News." <u>US News and World Report</u> 11 Jan. 1999: 16.

Editorial in a Periodical
> Fogarty, Robert W. "Fictional Families." Editorial. <u>Antioch Review</u> 56
> (1998): 388.

Letter Written to the Editor of a Periodical
> Paley, James A. Letter. "New Haven Renaissance." <u>New York Times</u> 30
> Jan. 1999: A26.

Review Article
If a review article has a title, add it after the author's name.

> Swain, William N. Rev. of <u>Getting Hits: The Definitive Guide to Promoting</u>
> <u>Your Website</u>, by Don Sellers. <u>Public Relations Review</u> 24 (1998): 403–09.

Presentation at a Professional Meeting or Conference
> Ciardi, John. Address. National Council of Teachers of English Conven-
> tion. Hilton Hotel, Washington, DC. 19 Nov. 1982.

Film, Slides, Videotape
Start with any actor, producer, director, or other person whose work you wish to emphasize. Otherwise, simply begin with the title of the recording. Note the form cited—videocassette, filmstrip, and so forth.

> <u>America in the Depression Years.</u> Slide program. Laurel: Instructional Re-
> sources, 1979.

> Olivier, Laurence, prod. and dir. <u>Richard III.</u> By William Shakespeare.
> Videocassette. London Film Productions, 1955.

> <u>Richard III.</u> By William Shakespeare. Prod. and dir. Laurence Olivier.
> Videocassette. London Film Productions, 1955.

> <u>Visions of the Spirit: A Portrait of Alice Walker</u>. By Elena Featherston.
> Videocassette. Women Make Films, 1989.

Programs on Radio or Television
   "Alone on the Ice." <u>The American Experience</u>. PBS. KRMA, Denver. 8 Feb. 1999.

   <u>The Life and Adventures of Nicholas Nickleby.</u> By Charles Dickens. Adapt. David Edgar. Dir. Trevor Nunn and John Caird. Royal Shakespeare Co. Mobile Showcase Network. WNEW, New York. 10–13 Jan. 1983.

CD or Other Recording
Identify the format if the recording is not on a compact disk.

   Basie, Count. "Sunday at the Savoy." <u>88 Basie Street.</u> Rec. 11–12 May 1983. LP. Pablo Records, 1984.

   Cherry, Don. "When Will the Blues Leave?" <u>Art Deco.</u> A&M Records, 1989.

Published or Personal Letter
   Lasswell, Harold. Letter to the author. 15 July 1976.

   Schneider, Alan. "To Sam from Alan." 3 Sept. 1972. <u>No Author Better Served: The Correspondence of Samuel Beckett and Alan Schneider.</u> Ed. Maurice Harmon. Cambridge: Harvard UP, 1998. 278–82.

   Thackeray, William Makepeace. "To George Henry Lewes." 6 Mar. 1848. Letter 452 of <u>Letters and Private Papers of William Makepeace Thackery.</u> Ed. Gordon N. Ray. Cambridge: Harvard UP, 1946. 335–54.

Published or Personal Interview
   Freund, Nancy. Telephone interview. 18 June 1998.

   Gerard, William. Personal interview. 16 May 1999.

   Previn, Andre. Interview. "A Knight at the Keyboard." By Jed Distler. <u>Piano and Keyboard.</u> Jan.–Feb. 1999: 24–29.

Computer Software
   <u>Biblio-Link II for Windows: Powerful Data Transfer for ProCit.</u> Diskette. Ann Arbor: Personal Bibliographic Software, 1993.

   Schwartz, Howard F., Robert Hamblen, and Mark S. McMillan, eds. <u>AG Photo CD-1.</u> Diskette. Fort Collins: Colorado State U and Advanced Digital Imaging, 1996.

Database Available On-line
   <u>Bartleby Library.</u> Ed. Steven van Leeuwen. 1999. 5 May 1999 <http://www.bartleby.com>.

Book, Article, or Other Source Available On-line
Besides author and title, add any translator or editor and the date of electronic publication or last update. Conclude with the date on which you

visited the electronic site where the source is located and the site's address.

Land-Webber, Ellen. <u>To Save a Life: Stories of Jewish Rescue.</u> 1999. 5 Feb. 1999 <http://sorrel.humboldt/edu/~rescuers/>.

Latham, Ernest. "Conducting Research at the National Archives into Art Looting, Recovery, and Restitution." <u>National Archives Library.</u> 4 Dec. 1998. National Archives and Records Administration. 5 Feb. 1999 <http://www.nara.gov/research/assets/sympaper/latham.html>.

Marvell, Andrew. <u>Last Instructions to a Painter. Poet's Corner.</u> 11 Nov. 1997. 5 Feb. 1999 <http://www.geocities.com/~spanoudi/poems/marvel04.html>.

Wollstonecraft, Mary. "A Vindication of the Rights of Women: With Strictures on Political and Moral Subjects." <u>Project Bartleby Archive.</u> Ed. Steven van Leeuwen. Jan. 1996. Columbia U. 5 Feb. 1999 <http://www.cc.columbia.edu/acis/bartleby/wollstonecraft>.

Magazine Article Available On-line

Chatsky, Jean Sherman. "Grow Your Own Employee Benefits." <u>Money.com</u> 30–31 Jan. 1999. 7 Feb. 1999 <http://www.pathfinder.com/money/moneytalk>.

Newspaper Article Available On-line

Wolf, Mark "Finding Art in Albums." <u>@The Post: World Wide Web Edition of the Cincinnati Post</u> 5 Feb. 1999. 5 Feb. 1999 <http://www.cincypost.com/living/album020599.html>.

Article from an Electronic Journal

Warren, W. L. "Church and State in Angevin Ireland." <u>Chronicon: An Electronic History Journal</u> 1 (1997): 6 pars. 6 Feb. 1999 <http://www.ucc.ie/chronicon/warren.htm>.

Electronic Posting to a Group

Faris, Tommy L. "Tiger Woods." Online posting. 3 Sept. 1996. H-Net: Humanities & Social Sciences Online Posting. 7 Feb. 1999 <http://www. h-net.msu.edu/~arete/archives/threads/tiger.html>.

Review Available On-line

Holden, Stephen. Rev. of <u>Anne Frank Remembered.</u> 22 Feb. 1996. 5 Feb. 1999 <http://www.english.upenn.edu/~afilreis/Holocaust/anne-frank-film.html>.

Public Web Site with Organizational Message

Raab, Jennifer J. "Greeting from Chairman Jennifer J. Raab." <u>Landmarks Preservation Commission New York City.</u> 8 Sept. 1998. 7 Feb. 1999 <http://www.ci.nyc.ny.us/html/lpc/home.html>.

Database or Other Source Available on CD-ROM
Use "n.p." to indicate either "no place" or "no publisher" if such information
is not available. Use "n.d." to indicate "no date."

> "Landforms of the Earth: Cause, Course, Effect, Animation." <u>Phenomena</u>
> <u>of the Earth.</u> CD-ROM. n.p.: Springer Electronic Media/MMCD, 1998.

> <u>Life in Tudor Times.</u> CD-ROM. Princeton: Films for the Humanities and
> Sciences, 1996.

APA (AMERICAN PSYCHOLOGICAL ASSOCIATION) DOCUMENTATION

The samples below show how to use APA style for citing a source in the text
and in the References section at the end of a paper.

APA Parenthetical Documentation   The basic APA parenthetical citation includes the author's last name and the date of publication, information generally sufficient to identify a source in the reference list. Although researchers
in the social sciences often cite works as a whole, the page number can be
added to identify exactly where a quotation or other specific information is
located. If the author's name is included in the text, it does not need to be repeated in the citation.

Single Author
> The city's most current traffic flow analysis (Dunlap, 1998) proposed two
> alternatives.

> Nagle (1998) compared the costs and benefits of both designs.

Two Authors
Use both names each time the source is cited. Use the word *and* to join them in
the text; use an ampersand (&) in parentheses and the reference list.

> Moll and Greenberg (1990) outline the advantages of a more flexible ap-
> proach to social context.

> An earlier study (Moll & Diaz, 1987) proposed classroom change as one
> research objective.

Three to Five Authors
Supply all the names the first time the source is cited. If it is cited again, use
only the name of the first author and *et al.,* for "and others."

> Greene, Rucker, Zauss, and Harris (1998) maintain that anxiety is an im-
> portant factor in communication.

> Greene et al. (1998) address anxiety and communication directly.

More than Five Authors

Use only the name of the first author with *et al.* in the paper, but supply the names of all the authors in the list of references.

Heath et al. (1988) continue to address the problems involved in implementing this methodology.

Group or Organization as Author

The Ford Foundation (1988) outlined several efforts to change decision-making processes.

Work without an Author

"Challenging the Myths" (1995) identifies several traditional beliefs about teacher training.

Page Numbers for a Work

The characteristics of successful charter schools follow an opening definition of the "charter school challenge" (Rowe, 1995, p. 34).

Two or More Works in the Same Citation

If several citations are grouped in one pair of parentheses, arrange them alphabetically.

Recent studies of small groups (Laramie & Nader, 1997; McGrew, 1996; Tiplett, 1999) concentrate on their interactions rather than their context.

Letters, Telephone Calls, E-mail Messages, and Similar Communications

These communications are personal and thus are cited only in the text, not in the references.

This staffing pattern for nurses is used at four of the six major metropolitan hospitals (G. N. Prescott, personal communication, August 23, 1999).

APA List of References   As you examine the following illustrations, notice how capitalization, underlining, punctuation, and other features change with the type of source noted. Note also that authors' names are listed with surnames first, followed by initials only. Although the entries in an APA reference list follow very specific patterns, references in your paper—to titles, for instance—should use standard capitalization. Similarly, the word *and* should be spelled out in your paper (except in parenthetical citations) even though the ampersand (&) is used in the references.

Book with One Author

Blau, T. H. (1998). <u>The psychologist as expert witness</u> (2nd ed.). New York: Wiley.

Nuckalls, C. W. (1998). <u>Culture: A problem that cannot be solved</u>. Madison: University of Wisconsin Press.

Several Works by One Author
List the works by year of publication, with the earliest first.

Muller, N. J. (1998). Mobile telecommunications factbook. New York: McGraw-Hill.

Muller, N. J. (1999). Desktop encyclopedia of the Internet. Boston: Artech House.

Book with Two Authors
Arden, H., & Wall, S. (1998). Travels in a stone canoe: The return to the wisdomkeepers. New York: Simon & Schuster.

Book with More than Two Authors or Editors
Greenfield, L. A., Rand, M. R., Craven, D., Klaus, P. A., Perkins, C. A., Ringel, C., Warchol, G., Maston, C., & Fox, J. A. (1998). Violence by intimates: Analysis of data on crimes by current or former spouses, boyfriends, and girlfriends (NCJ-167237). Bureau of Justice Statistics Factbook. Washington, DC: U.S. Department of Justice.

Hair, J. F., Jr., Anderson, R. E., Tatham, R. L., & Black, W. C. (1998). Multivariate data analysis (5th ed.). Upper Saddle River, NJ: Prentice Hall, 1998.

Work with a Group or an Organization as Author
American Public Transit Association. (1986). The 1986 rail transit report. Washington, DC: Author.

Amnesty International. (1998). Children in South Asia: Securing their rights. New York: Author.

Book without an Author
Ultimate visual dictionary of science. (1998). New York: Dorling Kindersley.

Work in a Collection of Pieces by Different Authors
Ombaka, C. (1998). War and environment in African literature. In P. D. Murphy (Ed.), Literature of nature: An international sourcebook (pp. 327–36). Chicago: Fitzroy Dearborn.

Collection of Pieces Cited as a Whole
Young, C. (Ed.). (1998). Ethnic diversity and public policy. New York: St. Martin's.

Work in Several Volumes
AFL-CIO. (1960). American Federation of Labor: History, encyclopedia, and reference book (Vols. 1–3). Washington, DC: Author.

Work Translated from Another Language
When you cite a translation in your paper, include both its original publication date and the date of the translation you have used, as in (Rousseau, 1762/1954).

Rousseau, J. J. (1954). The social contract. (W. Kendall, trans.) Chicago: Regnery. (Original work published in 1762.)

Work Appearing as Part of a Series
Frith, K. T. (Vol. Ed.). (1997). Counterpoints: Vol. 54. Undressing the ad: Reading culture in advertising. New York: Peter Lang.

New Edition of an Older Book
When you cite an older source in your paper, include the original publication date and the date of the new edition, as in (Packard, 1866/1969).

Packard, F. A. (1969). The daily public school in the United States. New York: Arno Press. (Original work published in 1866.)

Article in a Reference Volume
Breadfruit. (1994). In Crystal, D. (Ed.), The Cambridge encyclopedia (2nd ed., p. 175). Cambridge: Cambridge University Press.

Work Issued by a Federal, State, or Other Government Agency
Nelson, R. E., Ziegler, A. A., Serino, D. F., & Basner, P. J. (1987). Radioactive waste processing apparatus. Energy research abstracts Vol. 12, Abstract No. 34680. U.S. Department of Energy, Office of Scientific and Technical Information.

Reference to a Legal Document
Individuals with Disabilities Education Act (IDEA), 20 U.S.C. §1400 et seq. (1996).

Turner Broadcasting System Inc. v. Federal Communications Commission, 95 U.S. 992 (1997).

Article in a Journal with Pagination Continuing through Each Volume
Dinerman, T. (1998). The case for an American manned Mars mission. The Journal of Social, Political and Economic Studies, 23, 369–378.

Greene, J. O., Rucker, M. P., Zauss, E. S., & Harris, A. A. (1998). Communication anxiety and the acquisition of message-production skill. Communication Education, 47, 337–347.

Article in a Journal with Pagination Continuing Only through Each Issue
Brune, L. H. (1998). Recent scholarship and findings about the Korean War. American Studies International, 36(3), 4–16.

Special Issue of a Periodical
　　Larsen, C. S. (1994). In the wake of Columbus: Native population biology in the postcontact Americas. In A. T. Steegmann, Jr. (Ed.), <u>Yearbook of Physical Anthropology: Vol. 37</u> (pp. 109–154). New York: Wiley-Liss.

　　Riley, P., & Morse, P. R. (Eds.). (1998). Communication in the global community [Special issue]. <u>Communication Research, 25</u>(2).

Article in a Weekly or Biweekly Periodical
　　Greenwald, J. (1998, November 23). Herbal healing. <u>Time, 152,</u> 58–67.

Article in a Monthly or Bimonthly Periodical
　　Glausiusz, J. (1999, June). Creatures from the bleak lagoon. <u>Discover, 20,</u> 76–79.

　　Gordon, J. S. (1999, May/June). The great crash (of 1792). <u>American Heritage, 50,</u> 20–24.

Article in a Daily Newspaper
　　Levine, S. (1999, January 30). Hearing loss touches a younger generation. <u>The Washington Post,</u> pp. A1, A8.

Article with No Author
　　Fire and lightning. (1998, October 10). <u>New Scientist,</u> 25.

Editorial in a Periodical
　　Zuckerman, M. B. (1999, February 8). Coming to Russia's rescue. <u>U.S. News and World Report,</u> p. 68.

Letter Written to the Editor of a Periodical
　　Triebold, M. (1998, July/August). Digging bones for fun and $$$ [Letter to the editor]. <u>The Sciences,</u> 5.

Review Article
　　Glaeser, E. L. (1997, November). [Review of the book <u>Policing space: Territoriality and the Los Angeles Police Department</u>]. <u>Contemporary Sociology: A Journal of Reviews, 26,</u> 750–751.

Presentation at a Professional Meeting or Conference
　　Achilles, C. M., Keedy, J. L., & Zaharias, J. B. (1996, October). <u>If we're rebuilding education, let's start with a firm foundation.</u> Paper presented at the annual meeting of the University Council for Educational Administration, Louisville, KY.

Film, Slides, Videotape
If sources do not mention a place of publication, use *n.p.* If no date is mentioned, use *n.d.*

Biomes and habitat [Slides]. (n.d.). Los Angeles: Science Software Systems.

CityTV and Sleeping Giant Productions (Producers). (1994). Dalai Lama: A portrait in the first person [Videocassette]. n.p.: Films for the Humanities and Sciences.

Kotter, J. P. (Interviewer). (1982). General Foods Corporation: Interview Kenneth E. Fulton [Videocassette]. Boston: Harvard Business School.

Programs on Radio and Television
If appropriate, add the names of contributors or a specific episode before the series title.

The New Detectives: Case Studies in Forensic Science. (1999, February 9). Bethesda, MD: Discovery.

CD or Other Recording
Use *n.d.* and *n.p.* if you need to indicate that a recording or other source does not note the date or place of publication.

Cleveland, J. (1993). Marching to Zion. On The great gospel men [CD]. Newton, NJ: Shanachie Records.

Jamal, A. (1961). Night mist blues. On Ahmad Jamal at the Blackhawk [Record]. Chicago: Argo.

Nasser, G. A. (n.d.). Focus on Gamal Abdel Nasser: An interview with the former leader of the Arab world [Audiocassette]. n.p.: Center for Cassette Studies.

Letters, Interviews, and Personal Messages
If you have used a communication such as a letter in a print or other medium, follow the form for that type of citation. If the communication is a message or call not available to other researchers, cite it only in your text, not in your list of references. (See page 141.)

Paladichuk, A. (1998, August). Interview: Daphne Stannard, RN, PhD, CCRN: Families and Critical Care. Critical Care Nurse, 18(4), 86–91.

Terkel, S. (1996). On Big Bill Broonzy, interviewed by Studs Terkel. [Record]. n.p.: Folkways Records.

Computer Software
Weiss, H. J. (1990). PC-POM: Software for Production and Operations Management (Version 2.10) [Computer software]. Boston: Allyn & Bacon.

Database Available On-line
> Academic Info: Your Gateway to Quality Internet Resources [Database]. (1999, February 4). Retrieved February 5, 1999 from the World Wide Web: http://www.academicinfo.net.

Book, Article, or Other Source Available On-line
> Hornbeck, D. (1999, January 22). The past in California's landscape. California Mission Studies Association. Retrieved February 7, 1999 from the World Wide Web: http://www.ca-missions.org/.

> 1695: Northwestern Indians at Quebec; Huron intrigues. Collections of the State Historical Society of Wisconsin, 16. Retrieved February 5, 1999 from the World Wide Web: http://memory.loc.gov/cgibin/query/r?ammem/lhbum:@field (DOCID+Alit(M7689e42).

Magazine Article Available On-line
> All hope gone for Hussein, power is passing to Abdullah. (1999, February 7). Time Daily [Newsmagazine, selected stories on-line]. Retrieved February 7, 1999 from the World Wide Web: http://cgi.pathfinder.com/time/daily/0,2960,19381-101990206,00.html.

> Spragins, E. E. (1999, February 7). Patient power: How to beat job lock. Newsweek.com [Newsmagazine, selected stories on-line]. Retrieved February 7, 1999 from the World Wide Web: http://www.newsweek.com/nw-srv/focus/he/fohe0224_1.htm.

Newspaper Article Available On-line
> Harden, C., & Long, P. A. (1998, October 28). Grand jury begins work in bid probe. @ The Post: World Wide Web Edition of the Kentucky Post [Newspaper, selected stories on-line]. Retrieved February 5, 1999 from the World Wide Web: http://www.kypost.com/news/bids102989.html.

> Sack, K. On the bipartisan bayou, a brouhaha. (1999, February 5). New York Times on the Web [Newspaper, selected stories on-line]. Retrieved February 5, 1999 from the World Wide Web: http://www.nytimes.com/yr/mo/day/news/washpol/la-cooperate.html.

Article from an Electronic Journal
> Peiss, K. L. (1998, Fall). American women and the making of modern consumer culture. Journal for MultiMedia History, 1(1). Retrieved February 5, 1999 from the World Wide Web: http://www.albany.edu/jmmh/vol1no1/peiss.html.

Abstract Available On-line
> Gay, H. (1998 August). East End, West End: Science Education, Culture and Class in Mid-Victorian London [On-line abstract]. Canadian Journal of History, 33. Retrieved February 5, 1999 from the World Wide Web: http://www.asask.ca/history/cjh/ABS_897.HTM.

Electronic Posting to a Group
   French, M. (1996, February 21). Erie Canal? [Announcement posted on the World Wide Web]. American Society for Environmental History. H-Net: Humanities & Social Sciences Online Posting. Retrieved February 7, 1999 from the World Wide Web: http://www.h-net.msu.edu/~aseh/ archives/threads/eriecanal.html.

Database or Other Source Available on CD-ROM
   LandView III: Environmental mapping software. (1977). [Computer software]. Washington, DC: U.S. Department of Commerce; U.S. Environmental Protection Agency, National Oceanic and Atmospheric Administration: Bureau of the Census.

SAMPLE STUDENT PAPER (MLA STYLE)

Last name and page number 1/2 inch below top of page
Heading 1 inch below top of page
All lines double-spaced, including heading and title
Title centered
Title defines topic

Clara Lee

Professor Paul Smith

Writing Workshop II

5 May 2002

The Courage of Intimacy:

Movie Masculinity in the Nineties

Paragraph indented 1/2 inch or 5 spaces
1-inch side margins
Opening interests reader with detail from film

Mike Newell's 1997 film <u>Donnie Brasco</u> begins and ends with an extreme close-up of Johnny Depp's eyes. Shot in wide-screen so that the eyes literally span the entire screen, the image is a black-and-white snapshot that appears during the opening credits and returns as a full-color close-up at the end of the movie. Depp's lustrous eyes are large and black and beautiful, and gazing at them up close gives the viewer a surprisingly intimate sensation. Even within the conventional narrative that makes up the body of the movie, they become notice-ably important; Web-site critic Rob Blackwelder observes that "Depp

Quotation from electronic source
Support from print source

has [the central conflict of the movie] in his eyes in every scene," and Susan Wloszczyna of <u>USA Today</u> notes, "It's all in the eyes. Depp's intense orbs focus like surveillance cameras, taking in each crime and confrontation. He's sucked into the brutal, bullying lifestyle, and so are we." The close-up image at the beginning and end is one of the few instances in which the film draws blatant attention to its own style, but the device calls attention to the film's central focus, its constant prob-ing into the character at the center of the movie.

Somehow, without restricting the film to a first-person narration by Depp's undercover FBI agent, the audience comes to identify with him and understand the many pressures increasing inside his head

Lee   2

simply by watching his eyes. They reflect his watchfulness, his un-

certainty, his frustration, and his guilt—all without drawing too much

attention to himself from his unsuspecting wise-guy companions. He

is guarded with his words, causing his closest Mafioso friend to re-

mark, "You never say anything without thinking about it first." His

quietness invites viewers to read his looks and expressions, to be-

come intimately acquainted with a character who constantly has to

hide part of himself from the people around him, until they can virtu-

ally feel every twinge of fear or regret that the character feels. Seeing

this man trapped in situations in which he faces crisis after crisis, un-

willingly alienated from his family and eventually his employers, try-

ing only to protect the people he loves, viewers can ultimately recog-

nize him as a more sensitive, struggling, and courageous hero than

those celebrated in the past.

    Over the decades, Hollywood has glorified the gruff masculinity

of actors from Humphrey Bogart to Sylvester Stallone. Joan Mellen

notes in her 1977 book <u>Big Bad Wolves: Masculinity in the American</u>

<u>Film</u> that in traditional Hollywood films, especially the stoic action films

of the 1970s, "physical action unencumbered by effeminate introspec-

tion is what characterizes the real man" (5). In the 1990s, it seems

that much has changed; introspection has become a central part of

leading-male roles. Character-driven films of the past year alone have

won accolades for such intimate roles as Robert Duvall's tormented

evangelical preacher in <u>The Apostle,</u> Matt Damon's emotionally needy

genius, and Robin Williams' mourning therapist in <u>Good Will Hunting,</u>

and the unemployed guys struggling over issues like impotence and

child custody in <u>The Full Monty</u>. Thoughtfulness, vulnerability, and the

ability to handle relationships have become virtual requirements for

1-inch margin at top
Heading 1/2 inch
below top of page
continues last name
and page numbering

Quotation from film

Thesis stated

Past contrasted with
present

Source identified
in text

Quotation from book,
with page number

Other examples
noted

Background tied
to thesis

Lee   3

the male "hero" in the 1990s. The old-fashioned masculinity of charac-

ters played by Clint Eastwood or John Wayne in the past has come to

be regarded as emotionally repressed and overly macho.

The change is partly cyclical. Mellen cites the 1930s and 1950s

as eras in film in which leading men were given greater depth. She

Clarification added in brackets · says, "despite the limitations imposed by a repressive society [in the

fifties], film recovered for men an individual self with a distinctive

Quotation with two page numbers · identity and a flourishing ego" (191–92). Actors like Marlon Brando

and James Dean, in particular, played insecure, emotionally torn

rebels who express tenderness in their relationships with women and

with other men. However, in the sixties, "as the Vietnam War pro-

Ellipses for words omitted added in brackets · gressed [. . .] maleness itself appeared under siege and in need of

defense," and "traumatic events of the sixties induced the Hollywood

hero to tighten up, reveal as little about himself as possible, and to

find comfort in his own recalcitrance" (248–49). Things scarcely got

better when "glorification of the vigilante male [became] the dominant

masculine myth of the seventies" (295) with films like <u>Dirty Harry</u> and

Quotations and summary from source · <u>Taxi Driver</u>. "In the seventies film, people are allowed no option: they

must meet force with force" (307). Following two decades of grim

testosterone, there was a definite reaction in the bubble gum pop cul-

ture of the eighties, with flashy cartoon violence starring Sylvester

Stallone or Arnold Schwarzeneggar presenting highly unrealistic im-

ages of masculinity, and lighter portrayals like Marty McFly and Indi-

ana Jones gaining in popularity. By the nineties, American audiences

were no longer taking tough guy masculinity seriously, leading to a

trend of ironic humor in action films from <u>True Lies</u> to <u>Independence</u>

<u>Day</u>. It is doubtful that Will Smith would have been a favorite action

hero in any other era but the 1990s.

Lee   4

However, the crucial underlying shift in American culture is the

Transition back to present day

debilitation of the conventional white male hero in a country he once

monopolized. Trends in society within the last thirty years have led to

greater freedom for women, minorities, and homosexuals, and as

pride and power among these groups have increased, there has

been a backlash against the white male. Today's hero has to prove

that he is sensitive and completely respectful of every group men-

tioned above in order to remain sympathetic, forcing his previous role

of unquestioned dominance to change drastically. In addition, now

that women are going to work and less is expected of men in terms

of being the provider and protector of the family and society, more is

expected of them in their personal relationships. As noted recently by

Sylvester Stallone, a fitting symbol of the old macho masculinity who

is now trying to change his image to a more sensitive one, "I think the

Quotation from published interview

leading man of the future will be one who is beleaguered by the need

to constantly define on film the male-female relationship." He also

notes, "People want to nurture the underdog. The day of the strong-

man is over" (94). The themes of inefficacy in society, sensitivity in

relationships, and a reaction to the old strongman ideal show up

clearly in <u>Donnie Brasco</u>.

In the movie, FBI agent Joe Pistone, alias Donnie Brasco, goes

Analysis of film

undercover in the belief that he is on the side of law and order, with

the simple goal of booking some major criminals; instead he finds a

bunch of endearing but disturbingly violent men who become his

closest companions for several years. Particularly perplexing is his

relationship with Benjamin "Lefty" Ruggiero, the trod-upon hitman

Plot summary and interpretation

whose thirty years of faithful service are rewarded with dirty-work as-

signments while younger wise guys are promoted over him. Lefty is the one who notices Donnie and recruits him into the organization, and from the start his faith in Donnie is clear; as Pistone smugly reports to a contact early in the movie, "I got my hooks in this guy." However, Pistone's smugness wears off as Lefty repeatedly invites him into his home, confides in him with his complaints and his dreams, and says unexpectedly one day waiting in the hospital *Character analysis* where his own son is in the E.R. for a drug overdose, "I love you, Donnie." It is appropriate that the fictional Donnie Brasco is an orphan, because Lefty essentially becomes a surrogate father to him. Pistone, concerned for Lefty's fate, becomes more and more reluctant to "pull out" of his undercover assignment, revealing Donnie Brasco as a spy and leaving the blame (and death sentence) on Lefty. At one point he stops meeting his FBI contacts because they are pressuring him to pull out. Instead, he lets himself take on his mob alter ego more and more, tearing both his professional and personal lives apart.

In a way, the film is an interesting commentary on how ideals have changed, because it is set in the 1970s but made with a 1990s ideology. Because it is based on a book by the real agent Joe Pistone, who is currently living under the Witness Protection Program, one might think the portrayal would be strictly fact-based and would not be affected by the recent obsession with the sensitive male; but of course, one must never underestimate the power of filmmakers in any era to interpret their material with their own contemporary vision (note the portrayal of the Three Musketeers as aging and vulnerable in the recent screen adaptation of <u>The Man in the Iron Mask;</u> the seventies version of the same book depicted the Musketeers as brash and irreverent). There is plenty of traditional macho posturing in the Mafia sequences of

Lee   6

Donnie Brasco, but director Mike Newell places special emphasis on
Pistone's sensitive relationship with Lefty Ruggiero, his mentor in the
mob, and on his imperiled relationship with his wife. Newell, a British director most famous for his vastly different romantic comedy Four Wed-
dings and a Funeral, also boasted about Donnie Brasco's "absolutely
novel point of view about the Mob," focusing on "the lowest rung, the
have-nots" (Schickel), rather than the rich and powerful men at the top   *Electronic source*
so often depicted in mob movies. The film focuses on the soulful side of   *cited by author's*
a male protagonist in a genre in which sensitivity is rare.   *name only*

    In fact, Donnie Brasco has been recognized as "a different take
on the mob," an evolutionary step in the genre of gangster films. Time
calls it a "neo-Scorsesian study of lowlife Mob life" (Schickel), and
Blackwelder says that it "rises above the mire of its shopworn genre
by showing the cracks in its characters' armor." Chris Grunden sums
up the difference when he says, "Newell eschews fancy camera-work
and visual flair to remain tightly focused on the human drama—he's
made an actors' picture in a genre obsessed with style (GoodFellas,
Heat)." Conventional gangster films usually depict the rise and fall of a
charismatic criminal. The gangster movies of the thirties and forties
featured fast-talking tough guys like James Cagney and Humphrey
Bogart; Francis Ford Coppola's 1972 epic The Godfather, which re-
vived the genre, depicted the same glamour, ruthlessness, and power
of the Mafia, on an even greater romanticized scale. But after a spate
of stylized mob movies in the past twenty years, many reviewers of
Donnie Basco welcomed a new approach in a genre that was growing
old and stale. Put another way, Donnie Brasco is the film that finally   *Contrasts lead back*
brings its genre into the nineties by replacing its tough, glamorous   *to thesis*
hero with a real guy who can't live up to the stereotypes.

Almost in direct response to the ideal of masculinity presented in the past, Newall shows that although at first Pistone is doing every-thing right—fitting perfectly into his undercover persona, doing top-rate work for the FBI, and sending checks home regularly to his family—he cannot "be the man in the f—kin' white hat" that he thought he could be, as he puts it late in the movie. He knows how impossible it is to ful-fill his male responsibilities in all three of his very different worlds after he has ditched the FBI, almost lost his marriage, and realized that his undercover work, once revealed, will be the cause of Lefty's death. He has failed his own expectations of himself to save the day and make everything right. The contemporary audience recognizes the realism of the situation. As Stallone stated in his interview, "The male is [only] the illusion of the protector and guardian, [. . . b]ecause in this day and age, there is no security he can offer" (94). By now the audience real-izes that a hero cannot always save the day in a conventional sense. In an odd way, viewers even appreciate his failure because it has knocked all of his arrogance out of him and left only an exposed, vul-nerable character.

A contemporary audience can especially relate to the issues of family breakdown, recognizing in Donnie's situation the roots of the culture of estrangement and divorce which is so widespread today. Vi-olating the conventional lone male gangster/cop figure, Joe Pistone has not only a wife but three small daughters hidden away in subur-bia, and he can't tell them anything about his job without putting them at risk. His visits home are less and less frequent, sometimes months apart, due to the consuming nature of his "job." Although viewers can see from the start the tenderness and love he has for his wife and daughters, his prolonged absences and broken promises (he misses

Analysis of main character

Analysis of relationships with other characters

Lee   8

his daughter's first Communion) lead to intensifying arguments between him and his wife. As she constantly reminds him, his job is tearing their home apart, and not knowing what he is doing makes it all
the more unbearable. Pistone knows, as his identification with the
Mafia grows deeper and deeper, that his involvement has serious
consequences for his family, and this mounting pressure becomes impossible to resolve when weighed against the life of Lefty Ruggiero.

    Regarding the role of women in Mafia movies, Mellen points out *Contrasting example*
that "well into the seventies the male protagonist of films from The
Godfather (I or II) to Serpico uses women solely to discard them"
(327). Wives in The Godfather are cheated on, lied to, and in one
case, violently beaten. At a pivotal moment at the end of the movie,
the wife of Michael Corleone tearfully asks him if he has ordered the
death of his sister's husband, and he looks directly into her eyes and
lies, saying he did not. She smiles and believes him. Her character
is, in fact, constantly under the thumb of her husband who misleads
her, ignores her, and coaxes her into marrying him after not contact-
ing her for over a year. She and the other women in the movie are
not once consulted or listened to, no matter how much their hus-
bands' actions affect their lives.

    Donnie Brasco could have been made in precisely the same *Contrasting example*
way. Pistone's wife Maggie is, after all, left at home for months at a *related to film*
time while her husband is off doing his job for the FBI. However,
Newell makes the relationship between them a pivotal storyline in the
movie. Repeatedly in the course of the narrative, interrupting the
Mafia sequences, the audience sees Pistone call or visit home, reinforcing his identity as a husband and father. Viewers also note the
progression as his relationship begins to sour. The lowest point

*Incident from film
substantiates
interpretation*
comes when Pistone shows up at his home in the middle of the night
to retrieve a bag containing $3 million in cash and confronts Maggie,
who has found it and hidden it. When she tells him that he has become "like one of them," he strikes her, and both recoil in surprise,
less shocked at the blow that at the realization of what their marriage
has become. At this critical moment, he tries to tell her the truth. He
awkwardly explains the situation with Lefty and his fear of being responsible for his death. He tells her that he is not sure of what is right

Quotation from film
anymore. He tells her, "I'm not like them. I am them." It is evident that
the troubles of Pistone's marriage hurt himself as much as his wife,
and in a sense, dealing with them takes more courage than risking
his life as an undercover agent in the Mafia. The film treats this relationship delicately, and the woman here is not merely discarded or
lied to, but confronted and confided in, with her concerns presented
as clearly as his own.

What makes Pistone's situation so compelling is that he starts
out believing that he can be one of the traditional "solitary heroes

*Source identified
in citation*
who solve all problems for themselves" (Mellen 23) and instead
comes up against situations that are too difficult to handle. Joe Pistone slaps his wife, not to exert his male dominance, but because he
has lost control. When he tries to make things right, he doesn't
sweep her into his arms (and probably have his way with her, in the
true tradition of male heroes); he is almost frightened to make a

*Detail from
film supports
interpretation*
move and instead makes a gesture—kissing the back of her head—
to try and reestablish the emotional (not sexual) intimacy between
them. In his early scenes with Lefty, Pistone is noticeably on his
guard and detached from the affection Lefty is developing for him;
later, when he has the opportunity to be promoted within the ranks of

the mob and Lefty feels betrayed, Pistone tries to express his devotion by visiting him at the hospital where his son has overdosed. When Lefty orders him to leave, he refuses.

These gestures are some of Pistone's most heroic acts, at least as Newell presents it. Although he is given a medal and a check for $500 at the end of the movie for his undercover work (which is enough to secure scores of convictions), his feelings about it are clearly mixed; his loyalty to the FBI has been disintegrating as he has lost faith in their good guy/bad guy rhetoric, and his primary concern—Lefty's safety—is now uncertain. His success in infiltrating a group of depressed Brooklyn wise guys is now a cause for guilt. It is at this point at the end of the movie, as Pistone accepts his reward and his wife tells him it's all over, that Newell returns to the extreme close-up of Depp's eyes, and the audience sees how troubled they are. Viewers are left with that image, indicating that Newell intended for them to *Return to detail* leave the theater asking themselves what it was all for—whether doing *used in first* his job was really the right thing or not. True to life, there is no easy, *paragraph* happy ending, in which a man can die in battle or save the day and thus fulfill his "masculine" duties. What matters, however, as viewers return to that close-up, is that they have seen Joe Pistone/Donnie Brasco's vulnerability and his devotion within his relationships. If he feels confused or uncertain at the end, it is because he has faced these emotional issues, which are far more subtle than the challenges related to his job. The audience has seen him show more courage in *Return to thesis* his private struggles than John Wayne ever did out on the frontier and can applaud him for that.

*All lines double-
spaced, including
title and entries
Title 1 inch below
top of page and
centered
First line at margin
Next lines indented
1/2 inch or 5 spaces
Entries in
alphabetical order*

Works Cited

Blackwelder, Rob. "<u>Donnie Brasco</u>." Rev. of <u>Donnie Brasco,</u> dir. Mike

    Newell. <u>The Fairfield [CA] Daily Republic</u> 3 Mar. 1997: D5+.

    <u>Spliced Online</u> Archives Mar. 1977. 23 Sept. 1998 *<http://www.*

    splicedonline.com>.

<u>Donnie Brasco</u>. Dir. Mike Newell. Tristar, 1997.

Grunden, Chris. "<u>Donnie Brasco</u>." Rev. of <u>Donnie Brasco,</u> dir. Mike

    Newell. <u>Film Journal International Online</u> Mar. 1997. 20 Sept.

    1998 *<http://www.filmjournal.com/reviews/html/mar97 7.html>.*

Mellen, Joan. <u>Big Bad Wolves: Masculinity in American Film</u>. New

    York: Pantheon, 1977.

*Article title in
quotation marks*

Schickel, Richard. "Depp Charge," <u>Time Magazine Online</u> 3 Mar. 1977.

    22 Sept. 1998 *<http://cgi.pathfinder.com/time/magazine/*

    1997/dom/970303/depp.charge.html>.

Stallone, Sylvester. "Masculine Mystique." Interview. <u>Esquire</u>. Dec.

    1996: 89–96.

*Movie title
underlined*

Wloszczyna, Susan. "<u>Donnie Brasco</u>: A High Point for Lowlifes." Rev.

    of <u>Donnie Brasco</u>, dir. Mike Newell. <u>USA Today</u> 28 Feb. 1997: 1D.

Glossary of Literary Terms

Act   A major division of a play.

Action   What happens in a play or work of fiction.

Affective fallacy   The fallacy of wrongly evaluating a literary work by emphasizing only its emotional impact.

Allegory   A narrative whose characters, symbols, and situations represent elements outside the text. For example, the character Christian in the allegory *Pilgrim's Progress* represents the Everyman who is a Christian.

Alliteration   The repetition of consonant or vowel sounds at the beginning of words.

Allusion   An indirect reference to some literary or historical figure or event. For example, the line in T. S. Eliot's *Love Song of J. Alfred Prufrock*, "No! I am not Prince Hamlet, nor was meant to be," is an allusion.

Ambiguity   A literary device in which an author uses words with more than one meaning, deliberately leaving the reader uncertain.

Analogy   A comparison of two different things on the basis of their similarity.

Anapest   A metrical foot consisting of two unaccented syllables followed by an accented one (⌣ ⌣ /), as in the phrase "on the ship."

Antagonist   A competitor or opponent of the main character (protagonist) in a work of literature.

Antihero   A protagonist in a modern literary work who has none of the noble qualities associated with a traditional hero.

Antistrophe   In a Greek play, the portion of the Chorus that responds to the comments made by the first part of the Chorus, the Strophe.

Antithesis   A phrase that contains words whose meanings harshly contrast with each other and are in rhetorical balance. For example, Alexander Pope's "Man proposes, God disposes" is an antithesis.

Aphorism   A terse, sharp statement of a large principle or idea. Thomas Hobbes's "The life of man, solitary, poor, nasty, brutish, and short" is an aphorism.

Apostrophe   A direct, emotional address to an absent character or quality, as it if were present.

Archetype An Image or character representative of some greater, more common element that recurs constantly and variously in literature.

Aside Lines in a play that are delivered not to another character but to the audience or to the speaker himself or herself.

Assonance The use of similar vowel sounds in adjacent or close by words (for example, *slide* and *mind*).

Avant garde A term used to describe writing that is strikingly different from the dominant writing of the age—in its form, style, content, and attitude.

Ballad A poem originally sung or singable, recounting some domestic or heroic story, usually within a four-line stanza alternating three-beat and four-beat lines.

Bathos An unsuccessful attempt to arouse great emotion, becoming not grand but absurd or silly.

Blank verse Unrhymed lines of iambic pentameter.

Caesura A pause within a line of poetry, often created through punctuation.

Canon Those collective works generally considered by teachers, scholars, and experts as the most important ones to read and study because they qualify as "masterpieces" or examples of excellence.

Canto A division of certain long poems, such as Dante's *Divine Comedy* and Byron's *Don Juan.*

Carpe diem Latin for "seize the day," used in literature to describe poetry that examines temporary human pleasures against the backdrop of eternity—as in Marvell's "To His Coy Mistress."

Catharsis Exhaustion and cleansing of an audience member's emotions through participation in the events of a tragedy.

Character A person created by an author for use in a work of fiction, poetry, or drama.

Chorus A group of singers or actors who comment on and respond to the action in a play of classical Greece; also, a refrain in a song or poem.

Classicism A term deriving from the era of the ancient Greeks and Romans, used in English literature to describe the outlook of the eighteenth century, where writers celebrated the "classical" values of restraint, order, and stylistic elegance.

Cliché A phrase so overused that it has lost its original punch (for example, "beating a dead horse").

Climax A point at which the events in a play or story reach their crisis, where the maximum emotional reaction of the reader is created.

Coda A closing section of some literary works, occurring after the main action has been resolved.

Colloquialism A term used in speech but not acceptable in formal writing.

Colloquy A debate or conversation among characters.

Comedy A work of literature, often a play, whose first intention is to amuse and that ordinarily has a happy ending.

Comic relief A light, amusing section of a play or story that relieves tension and often comments by its humor on the surrounding serious action.

Complication   A part of a plot in which the conflict among characters or forces is engaged.

Conceit   A metaphor extended to great lengths in a poem (for example, Donne's "The Flea").

Conflict   A struggle among opposing forces or characters in fiction, poetry, or drama.

Connotation   Implications of words or sentences, beyond their literal, or denotative, meanings.

Consonance   Repetition of consonant sounds within words.

Couplet   Two lines of verse that have unity within themselves, often because they rhyme.

Crisis   The turning point in the action of a story or play.

Cue   In a play, words or action from one character that signal the start of another character's words or action.

Dactyl   A metrical foot containing an accented syllable followed by two unaccented syllables ($/ \smile \smile$), as in the word "craziness."

Denotation   Literal meaning of a word or of sentences.

Denouement   The final action of a plot, in which the conflict is resolved; the outcome.

Deus ex machina   Literally, "God from a machine"—the improbable intervention of an outside force that arbitrarily resolves a conflict.

Dialect   A type of informal diction spoken by a particular regional, social, ethnic, or economic group.

Dialogue   Conversation between two people in fiction, drama, or poetry.

Diction   The use of words; good diction is accurate and appropriate to the subject.

Dimeter   A line of poetry composed of two metrical feet.

Dionysian   A term referring to the ancient Greek values embraced by the god Dionysius and his worshipers—faith in the irrational and in the primacy of human emotions; often a descriptive term in literature.

Dramatic irony   A term used to describe the effect of words of a character in a play that have more significance than they appear to have.

Dramatic monologue   A poem spoken by a character other than the author (for example, Browning's "My Last Duchess").

Editorial omniscience   The entry of the narrator or author into a story in order to comment on a character or the action.

Elegy   A poetic meditation on death, often occasioned by the death of a specific individual.

End-stopped lines   Lines of poetry completed with the pause of punctuation.

Enjambment   Lines of poetry whose sense and grammar continue without a pause from one line into the next.

Epic   A long poem, usually narrative, recounting the trials and victories of a great hero, a hero usually important to an entire nation or people.

Epigram   A sharp, witty saying, such as Oscar Wilde's "I can resist everything but temptation."

Epigraph   A short inscription at the start of a literary work.

Epilogue   A concluding portion of a literary work, occurring after the main action has been completed.

Epithet   A descriptive word or phrase pointing out a specific quality—as when Shakespeare is referred to as "the Bard." The word is often used to describe terms of contempt.

Epode   The third portion of the comments of the Chorus in a classical Greek play, following the strophe and the antistrophe.

Essay   Literally, "attempt"—any short piece of nonfiction prose that makes specific points and statements about a limited topic.

Euphemism   A word or phrase substituting indirect for direct statement (for example, "passed away" in place of "died").

Euphony   A use of words to pleasant musical effect.

Exposition   An explanatory portion of a narrative or dramatic work that provides background and establishes the tone, setting, and basic situation.

Fable   A short tale that presents a specific moral and whose characters are often animals.

Fantasy   A work that takes place in a world that does not exist.

Farce   A broadly comic play relying for its humor on unlikely situations and characters.

Feminine ending   An additional syllable at the end of a line that has no metrical stress.

Figurative language   Language that deliberately departs from everyday phrasing, with dramatic and imagistic effects that move the reader into a fresh mode of perception.

First-person narrator   The "I" point of view in a story.

Foot   A metrical unit of a line of poetry that contains at least one stressed syllable and one or more unstressed syllables.

Foreshadowing   In a plot, an indication of something yet to happen.

Form   The structure and organization of a work of art; form expresses its content.

Free verse   Poetry that relies more on rhythm than on regular meter for its effectiveness.

Genre   A distinct kind of writing, such as mystery, gothic, farce, or black comedy.

Gothic fiction   Novels, often historical, in which weird, grotesque activity takes place; Mary Shelley's *Frankenstein* is an example of gothic fiction.

Haiku   A form of Japanese poetry now also practiced by Westerners, which in three lines of five, seven, and then five syllables presents a sharp picture and a corresponding emotion or insight.

Heptameter   A line of poetry composed of seven metrical feet.

Hero (or heroine)   The central character of a literary work; he or she often has great virtues and faults, and his or her trials and successes form the main action of the plot.

Heroic couplet   Two lines of rhyming iambic pentameter.

Hexameter   A line of poetry containing six metrical feet.

Hubris   Overbearing or insolent pride; in Greek drama, the arrogance toward the gods that leads to a character's downfall.

Humours   The four Renaissance divisions of human temperament, corresponding to the liquids of the human body—blood, yellow bile, black bile, and phlegm—which are often associated with the personalities of dramatic characters.

Hyperbole   Deliberately overstated, exaggerated figurative language, used either for comic or great emotional effect.

Iamb   A metrical foot composed of one unaccented syllable followed by one stressed syllable (˘ /), as in the word "undone."

Iambic pentameter   A line containing five iambic feet, the most widely used meter in English-language poetry.

Illusion   A false belief or perception.

Image, imagism   A concrete expression of something perceived by the senses, using simile, metaphor, and figurative language.

Internal rhyme   Rhyme that occurs within a single line of poetry.

Irony   An effect associated with statements or situations in which something said or done is at odds with how things truly are.

Line   The fundamental element of a poem—a set of words that ends at a specific point on the page and has a unity independent of what goes before and after.

Lyric   A short, personal poem marked by strong feeling, musicality, and vivid language.

Masculine ending   The last stressed syllable in a line of poetry.

Meditative poetry   Verse with a strong and personal expression of religious feeling, especially as practiced by John Donne and others in the seventeenth century; also, a form of poetry in which the poet muses quietly and personally on a particular scene or emotion.

Metafiction   A contemporary form of fiction in which an author makes the process of writing fiction part of his or her subject.

Metaphor   An implicit comparison of an object or feeling with another unlike it, as when Eliot's "Prufrock" says, "I have measured out my life with coffee spoons."

Metaphysical poetry   Thoughtful, often religious, intellectually vigorous poetry, as practiced by John Donne and others in the seventeenth century.

Meter   A rhythmic pattern in a poem created by the regular alternation of stressed and unstressed syllables.

Metonymy   A figure of speech in which an object or person is not mentioned directly but suggested by an object associated with it, as when a reference to "the White House" means "the President."

Mock heroic   A form of long poem in which the structures and values of the epic are used to burlesque a trivial subject (for example, Pope's "The Rape of the Lock").

Monometer   A line of poetry composed of only one metrical foot.

Mood   The emotional tone or outlook an author brings to a subject.

Muse   Originally any one of nine Greek goddesses presiding over the arts; "the muse" usually refers to an abstract being that inspires poets to write.

Myth   Ancient stories of unknown origin involving the supernatural myths have provided cultures and writers with interpretations of the world's events.

Narrative   A story that consists of an account of a sequence of events.

Naturalism   Literature in which the author attempts to represent the world in a realistic and often harsh and hopeless way.

Novel   A long fictional narrative that represents human events, characters, and actions.

Novella   A short novel or tale.

Octameter   A line of poetry composed of eight metrical feet.

Octave   An eight-line stanza of poetry, often part of a sonnet.

Ode   A lyric meditation, usually in elevated figurative language, upon some specific object, event, or theme.

Off rhyme   A form of rhyme employing not-quite-identical sounds, such as "slip" and "slap."

Omniscient narrator   A speaker or implied speaker of a work of fiction who can tell the story, shift into the minds of one or more characters, be in various places, and comment on the meaning of what is happening in the story.

Onomatopoeia   An effect in which a word or phrase sounds like its sense (for example, Tennysons's "murmuring of innumerable bees").

Ottava rima   An eight-line stanza whose end-words usually rhyme in an *ababababcc* pattern; used by many English poets (for example, Byron in *Don Juan*).

Pacing   Narrative or linguistic devices that keep literary works moving and interesting.

Parable   A story illustrating a moral, in which every detail parallels the moral situation.

Paradox   A statement that seems contradictory but actually points out a truth (for example, Wordsworth's line, "The child is father of the man").

Parody   A literary work that deliberately makes fun of another literary work or of a social situation.

Pathetic fallacy   The fallacy of attaching human feelings to nature.

Pathos   The qualities in a work of art that arouse pity or sadness, especially the helpless feeling caused by undeserved bad luck.

Persona   The mask through which a writer gives expression to his or her own feelings or participates in the action of a story, poem, or play.

Personification   A literary strategy giving nonhuman things human characters or attitudes, as in Aesop's fables or Keats's poem "To Autumn."

Plot   The sequence of events in a story, poem, or play; the events build upon each other toward a convincing conclusion.

Poetry   A form of writing in which the author writes in lines, with either a metrical pattern or a free-verse rhythm.

Point of view   The angle from which a writer tells a story. Point of view can be either omniscient, limited, or through the eyes of one or more characters.

Prologue   A preface or introduction setting the scene for what is to follow.

Prose   Any form of writing that does not have the rhythmic patterns of metrical verse or free verse. Good prose is characterized by tightness, specificity, and a sense of style.

Protagonist   The leading character; the protagonist engages the main concern of readers or audience.

Proverb   A statement putting forth a great truth (for example, the Biblical proverb "Go to the ant, thou sluggard; consider his ways and be wise").

Pun   A form of word play, often serious, that relies on the double meaning of words or sounds for its effect (for example, the dying Mercutio's words to Romeo, "ask for me tomorrow and you shall find me a grave man").

Quatrain   A four-line stanza.

Realism   An approach to writing that emphasizes recording everyday experience.

Refrain   A line or group of lines repeated several times in a poem.

Resolution   The dramatic action occurring after the climax of a play, before the events themselves are played out.

Rhetoric   The study and practice of language in action—presenting ideas and opinions in the most effective way.

Rhyme   Similarity of sound between words.

Rhythm   In poetry, the regular recurrence of stressed syllables; in literature in general, the overall flow of language, having a sensory effect on the reader.

Romance   Any work of fiction that takes place in an extravagent world remote from daily life.

Romanticism   A powerful literary movement beginning in the late eighteenth century; it shook off classical forms and attitudes, embracing instead the power, promise, and political dignity of the imaginative individual.

Satire   A literary work using wit, irony, anger, and parody to criticize human foibles and social institutions.

Scansion   The process of counting out the stresses that constitute the meter of a poem.

Scene   A portion of a drama, poem, or work of fiction that occurs within one time and setting.

Science fiction   Fantasy in which scientific facts and advances fuel the plot.

Sestet   A six-line stanza of poetry, often part of a sonnet.

Setting   The background of a literary work—the time, the place, the era, the geography, and the overall culture.

Short story   A brief fictional narrative.

Simile   A comparison of two things via the word "like" or "as."

Situational irony   The contrast between what a character wants and what he or she receives, arising not through the character's fault but from other circumstances.

Soliloquy   A speech by a character who is alone on stage, talking to himself or herself or to the audience.

Sonnet   A poem of fourteen lines using some kind of metrical form and rhyme scheme and always unified with a concentrated expression of a large subject.

Sound   In literature, the combination of sensations perceived by the ear or the mind's ear.

Spondee   A metrical foot containing two stressed syllables, as in the phrase "time out."

Sprung rhythm   A form of meter defined by the poet Gerard Manley Hopkins that emphasizes only the number of stresses in a line, thus making a kind of tense meter of accentual irregularity.

Stanza   A portion of a poem set off by blank space before and after; more formally, a stanza may have rhyme and metrical regularity matching that of stanzas before and after.

Stereotype   Widely believed and oversimplified attitudes toward a person, an issue, a style, and so on.

Stream of consciousness   Writing that attempts to imitate and follow a character's thought processes.

Stress   The emphasis a syllable or word naturally receives within a line of poetry, or in human speech.

Strophe   In an ancient Greek play, the comments of that portion of the Chorus speaking first during a scene.

Style   The property of writing that gives form, expression, and individuality to the content.

Subject   The person, place, idea, situation, or thing with which some piece of literature most immediately concerns itself.

Subplot   A complication within a play or piece of fiction that is not part of the main action but often complements it.

Subtext   Significant communication, especially in dialogue, that gives motivation for the words being said.

Surrealism   Art that values and expresses the unconscious imagination by altering what is commonly seen as reality.

Suspense   Those literary qualities that leave a reader breathlessly awaiting further developments with no clear idea of what those developments will be.

Symbol   Something that represents something else, the way a flag represents a country or a rose may stand for love—implying not only another physical thing but an associated meaning.

Synecdoche   A kind of metaphor in which the mention of a part stands for the whole (for example, "head" refers not only to the heads of cattle but to each animal as a whole).

Synesthesia   A subjective sensation or image (as of color) that is felt in terms of another sense (as of sound).

Synopsis   A summary of the main points of a plot.

Syntax   The arrangement of words to form sentences.

Tercet   A three-line stanza, often one in which each line ends with the same rhyme.

Terza rima   A series of three-line stanzas that rhyme *aba, bcb, cdc, ded,* and so on; used by Dante in the *Divine Comedy* and by Shelley, among others.

Tetrameter   A line of verse composed of four metrical feet.

Theater of the absurd Avant-garde, post-World War II drama representing the hopelessness of the human condition by abandoning realistic characters, language, and plot.

Theme The main idea of a literary work created by its treatment of its immediate subject.

Third person narrator The "he," "she," "it," or "they" point of view in fiction.

Tone The expression of a writer's attitudes toward a subject; the mood the author has chosen for a piece.

Tour de force A display of literary skill that is very impressive, but often empty.

Tragedy A literary work, usually a play, where the main characters participate in events that lead to their destruction.

Tragicomedy A work of literature, usually a play, that deals with potentially tragic events that are finally avoided, leading to a happy ending.

Trimeter A line of poetry containing three metrical feet.

Trochee A metrical foot consisting of an accented syllable followed by an unaccented one (/ ˘), as in the word "salty."

Understatement A passage that deliberately and ironically states or implies that something is less than it really is.

Utopia An ideal social and political state created by an author (for example, Plato, Thomas More, H. G. Wells, and Paul Goodman wrote about utopias).

Verbal irony The discrepancy between things as they are stated and as they really are.

Verse A unit of poetry, usually a line or stanza; in general, any kind of literary work written in lines.

Wit Originally a word that meant "intelligence," "wit" now refers to a facility for quick, deft writing that usually employs humor to make its point.

Permissions Acknowledgments

Index

I